T0213555

SpringerBriefs in Computer Science

SpringerBriefs present concise summaries of cutting-edge research and practical applications across a wide spectrum of fields. Featuring compact volumes of 50 to 125 pages, the series covers a range of content from professional to academic.

Typical topics might include:

- A timely report of state-of-the art analytical techniques
- A bridge between new research results, as published in journal articles, and a contextual literature review
- A snapshot of a hot or emerging topic
- An in-depth case study or clinical example
- A presentation of core concepts that students must understand in order to make independent contributions

Briefs allow authors to present their ideas and readers to absorb them with minimal time investment. Briefs will be published as part of Springer's eBook collection, with millions of users worldwide. In addition, Briefs will be available for individual print and electronic purchase. Briefs are characterized by fast, global electronic dissemination, standard publishing contracts, easy-to-use manuscript preparation and formatting guidelines, and expedited production schedules. We aim for publication 8–12 weeks after acceptance. Both solicited and unsolicited manuscripts are considered for publication in this series.

**Indexing: This series is indexed in Scopus, Ei-Compendex, and zbMATH **

Cătălin V. Bîrjoveanu • Mirela Bîrjoveanu

Secure
Multi-Party
E-Commerce
Protocols

 Springer

Cătălin V. Bîrjoveanu
Department of Computer Science
Alexandru Ioan Cuza University
Iasi, Romania

Mirela Bîrjoveanu
Vitesco Technologies
Iasi, Romania

ISSN 2191-5768   ISSN 2191-5776 (electronic)
SpringerBriefs in Computer Science
ISBN 978-3-030-99350-4   ISBN 978-3-030-99351-1 (eBook)
https://doi.org/10.1007/978-3-030-99351-1

This Springer imprint is published by the registered company Springer Nature Switzerland AG
The registered company address is: Gewerbestrasse 11, 6330 Cham, Switzerland

To our children,
Diana Andreea and Călin Paul

Preface

The rapid, widespread development of the digital world (Internet, communications, software, smart devices) is making traditional commerce obsolete and replaced by e-commerce, which is becoming a normalcy of everyday life. E-commerce is present when you want to do online shopping, pay a bill, pay taxes, or access a certain resource from a digital library. The usage on a large scale of e-commerce leads to new business models that require multiple parties to be involved. The widespread use of e-commerce in various ranges of applications opens up security breaches whose exploitation leads to major damage to all parties involved: customers, merchants, and e-commerce platforms. Thus, e-commerce protocols must provide protection against external attacks as well as from internal attacks initiated by one of the participants in the online transaction. Fairness is one of the key requirements that e-commerce protocols must guarantee. A customer who pays the merchant for a product wants to be sure that he will receive the paid product from the merchant. On the other hand, the merchant who supplies the product to the customer wants to be assured that he will receive the corresponding payment from the customer. When multiple parties are involved, guaranteeing fairness is much harder.

The main goal of this book is to develop secure multi-party e-commerce protocols which is a challenging issue because the extension from two-party to multi-party is a difficult task. The hardship of designing secure multi-party e-commerce protocols resides in multiple participants (customer, merchants, intermediaries, providers), the bundle nature of the goods purchased by the customer, and in the fact that some essential security requirements from two-party e-commerce scenarios are not preserved in multi-party e-commerce scenarios. In order to reflect the multiple possibilities in which the customer can place an order for online shopping, we consider complex transactions as combinations of aggregate, optional, and partial transactions. Optional transactions allow the customer to provide many preferences regarding physical products he wants to buy, aggregate transactions allow the customer to buy an entire pack of products, and partial transactions allow the customer to acquire only a part of a pack. Another topic covered in this book is the chained transaction in which the customer buys a physical product from a provider using many intermediaries.

The first step in designing secure multi-party e-commerce protocols is to adapt the definition of desired security requirements from two-party to multi-party. Some security requirements can be extended straightforward, but for fairness, effectiveness, and timeliness, we need to pay special attention. The main goal of the book is to provide multi-party e-commerce protocols that guarantee (among other security properties) strong fairness in complex transactions, chained transaction, and their combination, respectively.

The customer's privacy in complex transactions is another subject addressed in this book. Maintaining privacy of the customer brings new challenges: ensuring privacy for the customer in payment and in physical products delivery.

A chapter of this book is dedicated to formal verification of multi-party e-commerce protocols using AVISPA. This is an elaborate task due to the complexity of these types of protocols.

This book is mainly targeted at researchers and practitioners, particularly from the e-commerce security field and generally from the information security field. Further, it can be used as support for university courses in these fields. We believe that this book can be interesting for specialists in e-commerce who will find a starting point regarding secure e-commerce protocols involving multiple parties. This book can also be used by persons who have a general interest in e-commerce protocols because it offers state of the art and review for two-party and for multi-party fair exchange protocols.

Iaşi, România   Cătălin V. Bîrjoveanu
February 16, 2022   Mirela Bîrjoveanu

Contents

1 Introduction 1
   1.1 E-Commerce Types and Features 1
   1.2 Security Threats in E-Commerce 3
   1.3 E-Commerce Security Requirements and Protocols 4
   1.4 Challenges and Purposes of the Book 9
   1.5 Book Structure 11
   References 12

2 Two-Party E-Commerce Protocols 15
   2.1 State-of-the-Art Analysis 15
   2.2 Subtransaction Protocol 23
        2.2.1 Exchange Sub-protocol 24
        2.2.2 Resolution Sub-protocol 26
   2.3 Protocol with Physical Product Delivery Providing
        Customer's Privacy 27
        2.3.1 SPayment Sub-protocol 32
        2.3.2 SDelivery Sub-protocol 34
        2.3.3 Resolution Sub-protocols 35
        2.3.4 Security Analysis 37
   2.4 Comparative Analysis 39
   References 40

3 Multi-party E-Commerce Protocols for Complex Transactions ... 43
   3.1 State-of-the-Art Analysis 43
   3.2 B2B and B2C Use Cases 47
   3.3 Security Requirements 48
   3.4 Complex Transaction Protocol 49
        3.4.1 AggregateAbort Sub-protocol 54
   3.5 Complex Transaction Protocol Providing Customer's Privacy ... 57
        3.5.1 CTPCP Security Discussion 59

3.6   Comparative Analysis.. 61
References 62

4   E-Commerce Protocols for Multi-chained Complex Transactions 65
4.1   State-of-the-Art Analysis 65
4.2   Applications B2C/B2B 68
4.3   Security Requirements.. 69
4.4   Chained Transaction Protocol 70
    4.4.1   Resolution 1 Sub-protocol...................................... 75
    4.4.2   Resolution 2 Sub-protocol...................................... 77
4.5   Multi-chained Complex Transactions Protocol 78
    4.5.1   AggregateChainsAbort Sub-protocol 79
References 80

5   Formal Verification of Multi-party Fair Exchange
E-Commerce Protocols 81
5.1   AVISPA Tool 81
    5.1.1   High-Level Protocol Specification Language 82
    5.1.2   Verification Results Using AVISPA 90
5.2   Verification of Complex Transaction Protocols....................... 94
References 105

6   Conclusions 107

Chapter 1
Introduction

The e-commerce topic started in 1995. Since then, the widespread Internet access and rapid development of the technologies supporting the e-commerce infrastructure enabled a growing trend of e-commerce over the years. The current statistics reflect the continuing growth of e-commerce. According to *Eurostat: E-commerce statistics for individuals 2021* [14], 73% of Internet users in the EU shopped online in 2020. The report provided by *Insider Intelligence, eMarketer: Global E-commerce Update 2021* [10] shows that retail e-commerce had a continuous growth in 2020, with an average global growth of 27.6% compared with the previous year. Although the largest growth of 36.7% was in Latin America, China continues to lead the sales in the global e-commerce market with 2.779 trillion [10]. According to [15], analysts estimate that by 2023, digital transactions worldwide will trade $39 trillion. All these trends and estimates lead us to believe that in the next 10–20 years, most of the trade will be done through e-commerce.

Generally speaking, the term e-commerce includes any commercial activity which is performed partially or entirely online. Thus, e-commerce comprises online purchasing of physical/digital products and services, e-payment, e-procurement in supply chain, e-banking, e-gambling, e-auctions, and exchange of products and services.

1.1 E-Commerce Types and Features

E-commerce is very dynamic, being present in the everyday life of businesses, organizations, and individuals. E-commerce comprises a sum of different types of transactions conducted over the Internet. Depending on the actors involved in an e-commerce transaction, we can distinguish the following types of e-commerce:

- *Business-to-Consumer (B2C)* is the most common type of e-commerce. The commercial relationship is between an online business and the end user consumer.

© The Author(s), under exclusive license to Springer Nature Switzerland AG 2022
C. V. Bîrjoveanu, M. Bîrjoveanu, *Secure Multi-Party E-Commerce Protocols*,
SpringerBriefs in Computer Science, https://doi.org/10.1007/978-3-030-99351-1_1

B2C transactions include online retailers (e.g., Amazon) that sell products to consumers, content providers (e.g., Netflix) that sell online content to consumers, transaction brokers that help consumers to get the desired products, and service providers that sell services to consumers.

- *Business-to-Business (B2B)* is a transaction in which a business sells products to another business. B2B is the largest type of e-commerce in terms of revenues, including e-distributors (e.g., Amazon Business) that sell products and services to other business, industry consortium that serves specific industries, and e-procurement.
- *Consumer-to-Consumer (C2C)* is an online transaction allowing an end user to sell goods to another end user via online marketplaces such as eBay.
- *Consumer-to-Business (C2B)* is a transaction in which a consumer provides services for companies, including paid advertising on consumer Internet space (web site, YouTube, TikTok channel), promoting products on own blog, and providing reviews for products.
- *Business-to-Government (B2G)* refers to businesses supplying goods and services to government agencies. For example, a business bids for a contract for which a government agency launches a request for proposal.
- *Consumer-to-Government (C2G)* allows online transactions between consumers and government agencies, for tax payment, tuition fees, appointments for legal documents, information dissemination, and public consultation.

There are several key elements that make e-commerce attractive for use by individuals, businesses, and industry:

- Global availability and connectivity—E-commerce can be done anywhere and anytime using a wide range of devices that allow its functionality. The customer can buy products or services from home or work using his desktop or laptop or when he is on the move using his smartphone or tablet. The obvious advantage of e-commerce is the removal of proximity necessity for both seller and buyer, which leads to convenience and lower costs for doing business.
- Rich content—The content provided by e-commerce applications integrates video, audio, and text marketing messages, making the customers more informed about the products they are interested in.
- Interactivity—E-commerce systems allow merchants to communicate with customers in a manner similar to traditional commerce. Customers can interact with sellers, but also with other customers by posting comments, participating in discussion forums, or using social networks with functionality that allow information sharing.
- Personalization—In e-commerce, sellers can offer products and services tailored to the requirements, preferences, or previous purchases made by customers.
- Multitude applications support—E-commerce offers support for a wide range of applications like e-shopping, e-payment, e-procurement, e-banking, e-gambling, and e-auctions.

1.2   Security Threats in E-Commerce

E-commerce attracts more and more customers, businesses, and industries, as well as more criminals. It is much more simpler and with potentially fewer consequences to make crimes online than offline. For example, a cybercriminal can steal data, buy goods using fraudulent data, or shut down an e-commerce site and afterward disappears without a trace. So, a new challenge arises in e-commerce compared with traditional commerce: *security*. Unlike traditional commerce where the customer and the merchant are present face to face, e-commerce is performed using open networks (Internet) which are prone to security threats. The lack of a physically identifiable place where the customer can physically identify the merchant and vice versa leads to the loss of a valuable asset: *trust*.

In the following, we will present the most dangerous security threats for customers and merchants in e-commerce:

- *Phishing attacks* are usually done by sending spoofed messages to the victim via email or social media claiming to be from a legitimate party, such as the victim's bank, under the pretext of checking the victim's account (known as *spear phishing*). The purpose of the phisher is to trick the victim into revealing confidential information (such as bank account numbers, credit card numbers, PIN codes, and other personal information) or downloading malicious code like ransomware.
- *Card fraud/theft attacks*. Most e-commerce transactions are *card-not-present* (*CNP*), where the transactions are remote, meaning either the card, the cardholder, or the merchant is not present in the same place at the payment time. So, if a cybercriminal gains access to the victim's card data or card by theft, loss, or phishing, then he can use them to perform unauthorized transactions.
- *Identity fraud attacks* are realized by the cybercriminal impersonating the victim by using the victim's credentials (user name, password, banking data).
- *Sniffing attacks* involve network traffic monitoring with the aim to steal sensitive data including passwords, access codes, and card data.
- *Man-in-the-middle attacks* involve a cybercriminal that intercepts the communication between two parties, and also he can modify the messages exchanged between two parties by substitution, insertion, and deletion partially or entirely.
- *Denial-of-involvement attacks* appear when a participant denies its involvement in an e-commerce transaction. For example, a dishonest customer denies that he sent a purchase order to the merchant.
- *Denial-of-service attacks* are performed by flooding an e-commerce site with requests causing its shut down, so it is not accessible to authorized users anymore.
- *Insider attacks*. All the above attacks are not instrumented only by cybercriminals outside of the e-commerce platform. Also, we must consider that these attacks can be caused by participants from inside which act malicious or unaware employees.

Another form of attack that can interfere with e-commerce transactions is malicious code: viruses, worms, ransomware, and Trojans. Also, we must be aware of the security breaches that appear due to the underlying software of e-commerce applications that can lead to cross-site scripting, SQL injection, and cross-site request forgery attacks [18].

In the e-commerce protocols detailed in this book, we will consider a *Dolev-Yao intruder*, according to [9], with the capability to manipulate messages passing over the communication channels by deleting, replaying, and modifying, to masquerade as an honest participant, or to act as an inside honest participant. In [19], the following types of communication channels are defined: *operational*, where messages are correctly received in a finite amount of time; *resilient*, through which messages can be delayed but not lost; and *unreliable*, where the messages can be lost. Operational communication channels are too restrictive for the communication model of current networks (Internet). Thus, e-commerce protocols must take into consideration communication channels with fewer restrictions, such as resilient or unreliable, and also to solve the issues that may arise due to their use.

The *Seventh report on card fraud* issued by the European Central Bank in 2021 [13] analyzes data in 2019 regarding fraud using cards from *Single Euro Payments Area (SEPA)*, collected from 21 card payment schemes and payment service providers. According to [13], the total value of transactions using cards issued within SEPA and acquired worldwide increased in 2019 by 6.5% compared with the previous year, while fraud using cards grew by 3.4%, reaching 1.87 billion in 2019. Fraud in CNP transactions, meaning fraud in online payment transactions, continues the upward trend of the last 2 years, being the major component of fraud, reaching 80% of total fraud in 2019, with an increase of 4.3% compared to 2018. The widespread adoption of EMV smart cards by chip and pin technology [12] has led to far fewer opportunities for fraudsters compared to skimming and cloning fraud with magnetic stripe cards. Thus, in 2019, fraud at point-of-sale (POS) terminals is 15% of the total value of the fraud, while fraud at automated teller machines (ATMs) only 5% of the total value of the fraud.

All the security threats to e-commerce and the growing losses caused by them show the need for secure solutions and protocols to combat them. Only if the e-commerce environment will use solutions and protocols that guarantee a high degree of security, then individuals, businesses, and industries will gain enough confidence to use e-commerce and benefit from the advantages it offers without being harmed.

1.3   E-Commerce Security Requirements and Protocols

Next, we will discuss the security requirements that an e-commerce protocol needs to guarantee: authentication, authorization, integrity, non-repudiation, confidentiality, fairness, effectiveness, timeliness, and privacy. To highlight the need for these security requirements, we will consider in Fig. 1.1 a typical e-commerce transaction involving two parties: customer and merchant. In an e-commerce transaction, two

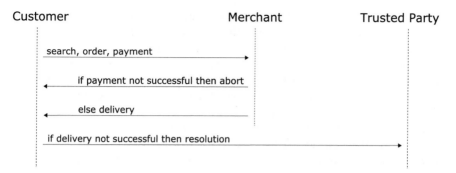

Fig. 1.1 Typical e-commerce transaction

phases can be identified: payment and delivery. In the payment phase, after the customer finds the product he is interested in, he sends a purchase order to the merchant and pays for the product. If the merchant receives the payment from the customer, then in the delivery phase, he sends the product (if it is digital) or a digital receipt (if the product is physical) to the customer. A dispute may arise between customer and merchant when the customer does not receive from the merchant the product (the digital product or a digital receipt corresponding to the payment for the physical product) he paid for. This dispute is resolved through a resolution sub-protocol in which the customer contacts a trusted (third) party agreed by the customer and merchant to restore the correctness of the exchange. The trusted third party can be the customer's bank or the payment service provider.

Entity Authentication allows one party to correctly identify the identity of another party. In an e-commerce transaction, the customer's bank must authenticate the customer on the payment data provided by him, to ensure that the customer that uses the card data is not a cybercriminal who impersonates the real cardholder.

Message (Origin) Authentication allows a party to ensure that a message comes from another party it claims to come from. In an e-commerce transaction, the payment service provider needs to verify the authentication of the payment request received from the merchant to ensure that it is not a counterfeit request from a malicious party.

Authorization determines what resources a user can access. For an e-commerce transaction, the customer's bank will approve or decline the use of the card by customer for a particular purchase transaction depending on the customer's authentication, customer's account balance, and specific conditions of the customer's account.

Integrity prevents unauthorized modification of data and is a consequence of the message (origin) authentication. If the payment service provider successfully authenticates the payment request he receives, then the integrity of data contained in the payment request is guaranteed.

Non-repudiation prevents that a sender (receiver) of a message can falsely deny that he has sent (received) the message. In e-commerce, the customer or the merchant can deny his involvement in transaction: a dishonest customer can deny that he sent a purchase order to the merchant; on the other side, a dishonest merchant can deny that he received the payment from the customer.

Confidentiality requires that the content of messages communicated between the participating parties is not accessible to unauthorized parties. An e-commerce transaction must protect the customer's payment information so that it is only disclosed to the customer's bank and payment service provider and it cannot be accessed by the merchant or any other malicious party.

Fairness. According to [4], two types of fairness are defined: *strong fairness* and *weak fairness*. A two-party e-commerce protocol ensures strong fairness if, after the protocol execution, the two parties will receive each other's items or none do. A two-party e-commerce protocol ensures weak fairness if it ensures strong fairness or the party who did not receive the item may prove to an external arbitrator that it sent his item to the other party. The environment in which e-commerce takes place makes that the customer and the merchant do not know each other and do not trust each other. It is essential that after the e-commerce protocol execution, a fair exchange has to be ensured: either the customer gets the digital product or a corresponding digital receipt (for a physical product) and the merchant gets the payment for product, or none do. An e-commerce protocol must prevent cases of unfair exchange or restore fairness if such cases occur. An unfair case in which the customer is harmed appears when the customer pays to the merchant, but the merchant does not deliver the product (digital product or the digital receipt) to the customer. Also, an unfair case in which the merchant can be harmed appears if the merchant delivers the product to the customer, but without the customer having paid for the product. Thus, in such unfair situations, the e-commerce protocol must have sufficient evidences so that the honest party can demonstrate to the trusted third party the dishonest behavior of the other party. Strong fairness requires a fair exchange obtained within the protocol, while weak fairness is achieved by resolving a dispute outside the protocol, such as court of law. Obviously, both the customer and the merchant will want to use e-commerce protocols that guarantee strong fairness.

E-commerce protocols assuring fairness (known as fair exchange e-commerce protocols) are used in different e-commerce transactions depending on the items exchanged between parties, such as:

- *Purchase*,
    - Electronic payment for digital receipt: the customer exchanges an electronic payment for a digital receipt (corresponding to a physical product/service) from the merchant
    - Electronic payment for digital product/service: the customer exchanges an electronic payment for a digital product/service of the merchant

- *Contract signing*: the customer exchanges his digital signature on a contract for the merchant's signature on the contract

- *Barter*: a party exchanges an arbitrary item of value for another item of value from the other party
- *Certified email*: a party (sender) exchanges an email for an acknowledgment receipt from another party (receiver)

E-commerce protocols proposed in the literature for obtaining fairness can be classified into two categories depending on the use of a trusted third party (*TTP*): protocols without *TTP* and protocols with *TTP*.

E-commerce protocols in the first category are further divided into gradual exchange, probabilistic, and smart contract-based protocols. Gradual exchange protocols (e.g., the one proposed in [7]) can be applied if two parties want to exchange items that can be divided into small parts, where the small parts are useful in themselves. The micro-payment schemes [25] are examples of gradual exchange protocols: the exchange takes place in many rounds, the customer paying in each round a small amount for a small part of the video from the merchant. The probabilistic protocols, such as the one proposed in [16], use the same way of sending a bit of item in each round, but they gradually increase the probability of reaching fairness. In [20], it has been proved that gradual exchange and probabilistic protocols cannot obtain fairness without *TTP*. In [2], a delivery smart contract-based protocol is proposed, which uses Ethereum blockchain and a delivery smart contract through which the customer buys a physical product from the merchant. The smart contract has the role to enforce the fair application of the payment transaction. But, this protocol does not guarantee fairness, because after the customer makes the payment, it may receive a different product than the one he paid for. Thus, the protocols proposed so far from this category do not guarantee fairness.

To achieve fairness, e-commerce protocols based on *TTP*, which belong to the second category, were proposed. In these protocols, *TTP* is used to solve any dispute or as an item validator. Depending on the degree of *TTP*'s involvement, *TTP*-based e-commerce protocols are further divided into fair exchange protocols with inline *TTP* (where *TTP* is used in every protocol's message), fair exchange protocols with online *TTP* (in which *TTP* is involved in every protocol's instance), and fair exchange protocols with offline *TTP* (where *TTP* intervenes only if a dispute arises). For efficiency and security reasons, the fair exchange protocols with offline *TTP* (also called optimistic fair exchange protocols) are preferred. In the inline or online *TTP*-based protocols, *TTP* can become a bottleneck leading to denial-of-service attacks. In literature, strong fairness is guaranteed by e-commerce protocols for the exchange of an electronic payment for a digital product: with online *TTP* [22] and optimistic [1, 21]. Also, strong fairness is obtained in e-commerce protocols for the exchange between the electronic payment and a physical product: with online *TTP* [27] and optimistic [8].

Effectiveness is ensured if every party involved in protocol behaves honestly (according to the protocol's rules) and no communication error occurs; then after protocol execution, each party will receive the item from the other party, without *TTP* involvement. Effectiveness is satisfied by optimistic fair exchange protocols.

Timeliness is ensured if each party involved in protocol behaving honestly is confident that the protocol execution will be completed in a certain finite time and fairness obtained after the completion of the protocol cannot be decreased. An e-commerce protocol must guarantee to an honest customer who paid for a product to the merchant, but did not receive the product, that he will receive the product or recover his money by a resolution sub-protocol that will be completed in finite time.

Customer's Privacy [3] includes two requirements: *customer's anonymity* and *customer's transaction unlinkability*. In e-commerce, customer's anonymity is important because the customer does not want to reveal to the unauthorized parties (e.g., merchant) information like his real identity, credit card number, or bank account number. Customer's transaction unlinkability guarantees that no unauthorized party can link the customer and the transactions in which he is involved. Customer's privacy does not allow the merchant to build the customer's purchase profile that can later be used for commercial purposes. Customer's privacy and strong fairness are provided by e-commerce protocols for buying digital products: with online *TTP* [17] and optimistic [23]. For buying physical products, e-commerce protocols are proposed: with online *TTP* [5] assuring customer's privacy and strong fairness and optimistic [2] assuring customer's privacy.

3-D Secure Protocol was initially developed in 2001 by Visa as *Verified by Visa* program [26], to enable authentication of customers to their card issuer during CNP e-commerce transactions, and was later adopted also by Mastercard, Discover, and American Express. *3-D Secure* is widely used in practice having a global average acceptance rate of around 77% [24].

Visa [26] has developed the *three-domain model* (*3-D model*) of a payment system that consists of issuer, acquirer, and interoperability domains. The issuer domain is composed of the customer (cardholder) and his bank (issuer). The customer's bank operates an *Access Control Server* (*ACS*) to perform customer's authentication. The acquirer domain consists of the merchant and his bank (acquirer). The merchant has a *merchant plug-in* (*MPI*) used as an interface between merchant and *VisaNet*. The interoperability domain is operated by Visa, including a *Visa Directory Server* (*VDS*) that allows the issuer and acquirer domains to interoperate globally. *3-D Secure Protocol* requires the communication channels between customer and merchant, customer and *ACS*, merchant and *VDS*, and *VDS* and *ACS* to be secured through SSL (Secure Sockets Layer)/TLS (Transport Layer Security) protocol. The customer initiates *3-D Secure Protocol* by sending to the merchant the purchase order including his payment information. *MPI* sends a request to *VDS* to verify if the cardholder is enrolled in *Verified by Visa*. *VDS* forwards the request to *ACS* to determine whether authentication is available for the card. The response received from *ACS* is forwarded by *VDS* to *MPI*. If the customer is enrolled, then *MPI* contacts *ACS* to authenticate the customer by providing his credentials (usually a one-time password and a static password). If the customer's authentication is successful, then *MPI* sends an authorization request to the acquirer, which in turn sends it to the issuer through *VisaNet*. The protocol ensures customer's authentication and authorization, integrity, non-repudiation, confidentiality, weak fairness (the disputes are solved outside the protocol), effectiveness, and timeliness.

A new specification of the protocol, *EMV 3-D Secure* (v2.0.0), was released in 2016 by EMVCo [11]. Currently, *Visa Secure* (former named *Verified by Visa*) is Visa's implementation of *EMV 3-D Secure*.

1.4 Challenges and Purposes of the Book

Up to now, in the literature, a high amount of effort has been dedicated to two-party e-commerce protocols (in which only one customer and one merchant are involved) and to multi-party e-commerce protocols for digital signature of contracts, non-repudiation, exchange of digital items, and certified email. Nowadays, many e-commerce applications involving online shopping require multiple parties. The work dedicated to multi-party solutions for complex transactions where a customer wants to buy several physical products from different merchants started in 2018 [6]. In this book, we continue and extend our research on this interesting topic. An example of an application requiring multiple parties is when a customer wants to buy a package of physical products consisting of several products that can be purchased from several merchants. The customer may be interested in buying either all the products in the package or none (this scenario corresponds to the aggregate e-commerce transactions). On the other hand, the customer may be interested in purchasing as many products as possible from the package, not necessarily all of them. This scenario corresponds to the partial e-commerce transactions which are applicable when the customer wants to buy products from certain preferred merchants, and for the other products in the package left to buy, he might find other alternatives (merchants). Also, to add even more flexibility to the way the customer can purchase products, the customer may want a package of products in which one or more of them are not necessarily individual products. Thus, a component (or more components) of the package may in turn be a package (corresponding to an aggregate or partial transaction) or may be a specification of preferences by which the customer wishes to buy exactly one of the products specified according to his preferences (the scenario corresponds to optional e-commerce transactions). We consider that complex transactions defined as combinations in any form of aggregate, optional, and partial transactions capture the most diverse way in which the customer can place an order for online shopping.

Regarding fairness in complex transactions, several issues may arise that in two-party transactions do not occur. For example, in an aggregate transaction which is a component of a complex transaction, the customer can successfully purchase only a part of the products in the pack and not all of them (e.g., due to lack of stock). In this case, the fairness for the aggregate transaction is not satisfied, although the fairness for all transactions involving the component products in the package is ensured. Another issue can appear in an optional transaction from a complex transaction in which the customer can successfully purchase more than one product from the pack and not only one of them. Although the fairness for all transactions involving the component products in the pack can be guaranteed, the fairness for the optional transaction is not assured. Ensuring fairness is a challenging issue in environments where multiple parties are involved, such as online shopping. The main goal of the book is to provide multi-party e-commerce protocols that guarantee strong fairness in complex transactions which allow the acquisition of physical products.

Ensuring privacy of customer is another important requirement in e-commerce. This is a challenge when the customer wants to buy physical products online. If in e-commerce transactions sensitive information about the customer related to his identity (his name, his address, his banking info), his involvement in transactions, can be known by the merchant, then the latter can use them to build the customer's profile. Another purpose of the book is to provide privacy for the customer in multi-party e-commerce protocols in which the customer wants to purchase physical products in complex transactions. For this aim, two main issues must be solved: ensuring privacy for the customer when he pays for the products in the pack and also when he collects the physical products.

When the customer buys a physical product from a merchant, either the merchant is the provider of the product or has purchased it in turn from another merchant (which may or not be the product's producer). In this multi-party e-commerce model, participants can play a new role, intermediary, which corresponds to on-demand e-commerce transactions in which the intermediary purchases a physical product only if he receives a purchase request for it from a customer or another intermediary. These scenarios require consideration of a new type of multi-party e-commerce transaction in which the customer buys a physical product from a provider through many intermediaries. These chained transactions are a particular case of supply chains. Ensuring strong fairness in chained transactions is a challenging issue because an intermediary can buy a product on demand without being able to provide it to the customer or intermediary who requested it (due to insufficient funds or malicious behavior of the party requesting the product). In this case, the fairness for the chained transaction is not satisfied, although the fairness for all two-party transactions belonging to the chained transaction is guaranteed. We can make a step forward in obtaining multi-chained complex e-commerce transactions by combining the complex transactions and chained transactions, in which the customer wants to buy physical products in complex transactions and each product is acquired in a chained transaction. Consequently, another objective is to describe multi-party e-commerce protocols that provide strong fairness in chained and multi-chained complex transactions.

Extending from two-party to multi-party e-commerce scenarios causes certain security requirements to change. Thus, in order to have a uniform picture of the security requirements provided by the two types of scenarios and the implications of this extension, we have to adapt the security requirements defined in Sect. 1.3 for two-party scenarios.

Designing efficient multi-party e-commerce protocols is one of our goals. The efficiency of a multi-party protocol depends on the number of protocol's messages, the complexity of the messages regarding the number of cryptographic operations applied, the degree of involvement of TTP, the number of participants, and their degree of involvement in resolution. The efficiency of multi-party protocols is not easy to achieve when applied in complex scenarios, such as those covered in the book. Also, the efficiency must not affect the level of security that the protocol provides.

Formal verification of multi-party protocols is essential because it gives greater confidence to the parties involved in using such protocols. The complexity of multi-party protocols makes their formal verification a difficult task.

This book is mainly targeted to researchers and practitioners from the field of information security, especially from e-commerce security, while also providing support for university courses in these fields. Any specialist in the e-commerce domain who wants to design secure e-commerce multi-party applications will find a starting point in this book.

1.5   Book Structure

This book consists of six main chapters. Next, we briefly describe the chapters.

Chapter 2 presents the state of the art and review of two-party e-commerce protocols that provide fair exchange between the payment and digital/physical products. Also, solutions that ensure the privacy of customer in these e-commerce systems are discussed. We present in detail an e-commerce protocol used when a customer buys a physical product from a merchant and an e-commerce protocol with physical product delivery that provides the customer's privacy. The chapter includes a comparative analysis of the existing solutions regarding both types of products (digital and physical) involved in the e-commerce transaction, as well as regarding the security requirements they provide.

Chapter 3 begins with the presentation and analysis of the current multi-party fair exchange protocols with various applications in e-commerce. The discussion emphasizes the lack of efficient solutions ensuring the customer's privacy in an important type of multi-party e-commerce transactions: complex transactions. After the discussion from the previous chapter, a new challenge arises: how to design e-commerce protocols that ensure fairness and customer's privacy in multi-party scenarios, as long as the two-party e-commerce protocols are not appropriate and cannot be easily extended to multi-party scenarios? Fairness and customer's privacy in complex transactions are challenging issues that we approach in this chapter. Two solutions for multi-party scenarios are detailed in this chapter: a fair exchange e-commerce protocol for complex transactions in which the customer buys several different physical products from different merchants and an e-commerce protocol for physical products delivery in complex transactions that provides fair exchange and the customer's privacy. Both solutions are analyzed, and a comparative analysis between these solutions and the existing ones is provided. Use cases of the solutions detailed in this chapter are presented for B2B and B2C scenarios.

In Chap. 4, we describe the state-of-the-art analysis regarding multi-party fair exchange e-commerce protocols considering intermediaries. This chapter highlights the issues that arise with regard to fairness in chained transactions and details a chained transaction e-commerce protocol. Starting from the business models that include complex transactions and chained transaction independently, we naturally extend them to a business model which takes into consideration both complex and chained transactions obtaining multi-chained complex transaction. Then, we are focusing on an e-commerce protocol for multi-chained complex transactions.

Chapter 5 provides an overview of the AVISPA tool for automated validation of large-scale Internet security protocols. The chapter presents the architecture of the AVISPA tool, the four back-ends from AVISPA with the main focus on the Cl-AtSe model checker, and the High-Level Protocol Specification Language (HLPSL). A security protocol for authenticated session key distribution is used as an example for specification and explanations regarding its verification using Cl-AtSe. This chapter also includes the formal verification using Cl-AtSe of the multi-party fair exchange e-commerce protocols proposed in the previous chapter. The Complex Transaction Protocol and the Chained Transaction Protocol are large multi-party protocols; therefore, their formal proof is a challenging issue. The complexity of multi-party protocols makes their formal verification a difficult task. The verification results obtained using Cl-AtSe demonstrate that all security requirements of the proposed multi-party e-commerce protocols are met.

Chapter 6 analyzes the efficiency of the multi-party e-commerce protocols detailed in this book. This chapter also summarizes their benefits and implications in e-business.

References

1. Alaraj, A., Munro, M.: An e-commerce fair exchange protocol that enforces the customer to be honest. Int. J. Prod. Lifecycle Manag. **3**(2/3), 114–131 (2008)
2. AlTawy, R., ElSheikh, M., Youssef, A.M., Gong, G.: Lelantos: a blockchain-based anonymous physical delivery system. In: 15th Annual Conference on Privacy, Security and Trust (PST), pp. 15–1509 (2017). https://doi.org/10.1109/PST.2017.00013
3. Androulaki, E.: A Privacy Preserving E Commerce Oriented Identity Management Architecture. PhD Thesis, Columbia University (2011)
4. Asokan, N., Schunter, M., Waidner, M.: Optimistic protocols for fair exchange. In: Proceedings of the 4th ACM Conference on Computer and Communications Security, pp. 7–17 (1997). https://doi.org/10.1145/266420.266426
5. Bîrjoveanu, C.V.: Anonymity and fair-exchange in e-commerce protocol for physical products delivery. In: Proceedings of the 12th International Conference on Security and Cryptography—SECRYPT, (ICETE 2015), pp. 170–177. SCITEPRESS (2015). https://doi.org/10.5220/0005508801700177
6. Bîrjoveanu, C.V., Bîrjoveanu, M.: An optimistic fair exchange e-Commerce protocol for complex transactions. In: 15th International Joint Conference on e-Business and Telecommunications, ICETE 2018—vol. 2. SECRYPT, pp. 111–122. SCITEPRESS (2018). https://doi.org/10.5220/0006853502770288
7. Damgård, I.B.: Practical and provably secure release of a secret and exchange of signatures. In: Helleseth, T. (ed.) Advances in Cryptology—EUROCRYPT 1993. Lecture Notes in Computer Science, vol. 765. Springer, Berlin, Heidelberg (1994). https://doi.org/10.1007/3-540-48285-7_17

8. Djuric, Z., Gasevic, D.: FEIPS: A secure fair-exchange payment system for internet transactions. Comput. J. **58**(10), 2537–2556 (2015)

9. Dolev, D., Yao, A.: On the security of public-key protocols. IEEE Trans. Inform. Theory **2**(29), 198–208 (1983). https://doi.org/10.1109/TIT.1983.1056650

10. eMarketer, Insider Intelligence: Global Ecommerce Update 2021. https://www.emarketer.com/content/global-ecommerce-update-2021. Cited June 25, 2022

11. EMVCo.: EMV 3-D Secure Protocol and Core Functions Specification. Version 2.3.0.0 (2021). https://www.emvco.com/emv-technologies/3d-secure/. Cited June 25, 2022

12. EMVCo.: Worldwide EMV Deployment Statistics (2021) https://www.emvco.com/about/deployment-statistics/. Cited June 25, 2022

13. European Central Bank: Seventh report on card fraud (2021) https://www.ecb.europa.eu/pub/cardfraud/html/ecb.cardfraudreport202110~cac4c418e8.en.html Cited June 25, 2022

14. Eurostat—Statistics Explained: E-commerce statistics for individuals 2021 https://ec.europa.eu/eurostat/statistics-explained/index.php?title=E-commerce_statistics_for_individuals. Cited June 25, 2022

15. Laudon, K.C., Traver, C.G.: E-Commerce 2021–2022 Business. Technology. Society, 17th edn. Pearson (2021)

16. Markowitch, O., Roggeman, Y.: Probabilistic non-repudiation without trusted third party. In: Proceedings of the Conference on Security in Communication Networks (1999)

17. Mars, A., Adi, W.: Fair exchange and anonymous E-commerce by deploying clone-resistant tokens. In: 2019 42nd International Convention on Information and Communication Technology, Electronics and Microelectronics (MIPRO), pp. 1226–1231 (2019). https://doi.org/10.23919/MIPRO.2019.8756734

18. MITRE Corporation: 2021 Common Weakness Enumeration (CWE) Top 25 Most Dangerous Software Weaknesses. https://cwe.mitre.org/top25/archive/2021/2021_cwe_top25.html Cited June 25, 2022

19. Onieva, J.A., Lopez, J., Zhou, J.: Secure Multi-Party Non-Repudiation Protocols and Applications. Springer, Berlin (2009)

20. Pagnia, H., Gärtner, F.: On the impossibility of fair exchange without a trusted third party. Technical Report TUD-BS-1999-02, University of Darmstadt, Germany (1999)

21. Ray, I., Ray, I.: An optimistic fair exchange e-commerce protocol with automated dispute resolution. In: Proceedings of 1st Electronic Commerce and Web Technologies Conference EC-Web 2000. Lecture Notes in Computer Science, vol. 1875, pp. 84–93. Springer, Berlin (2000)

22. Ray, I., Ray, I., Narasimhamurthi, N.: A fair-exchange e-commerce protocol with automated dispute resolution. In: Proceedings of the 14th Annual IFIP WG 11.3 Working Conference on Database Security, The Netherlands, pp. 27–38 (2001)

23. Ray, I., Ray, I., Narasimhamurthy, N.: An anonymous failure resilient fair-exchange ecommerce protocol. Decis. Support Syst. **39**(3), 267–292 (2005)

24. Ravelin: Why do 3D Secure acceptance rates vary by country and how can you manage this? https://www.ravelin.com/blog/why-do-3d-secure-acceptance-rates-vary-by-country-and-how-can-you-manage-this Cited June 25, 2022

25. Rivest R.L., Shamir, A.: PayWord and MicroMint: two simple micropayment schemes. In: Lomas, M. (ed.) Security Protocols 1996. Lecture Notes in Computer Science, vol 1189. Springer, Berlin, Heidelberg (1997). https://doi.org/10.1007/3-540-62494-5_6

26. Visa: Verified by Visa Acquirer and Merchant Implementation Guide. (2011) https://usa.visa.com/dam/VCOM/download/merchants/verified-by-visa-acquirer-merchant-implementation-guide.pdf. Cited June 25, 2022

27. Zhang, Q., Markantonakis, K., Mayes, K.: A practical fair exchange e-payment protocol for anonymous purchase and physical delivery. In: Proceedings of the 4th ACS/IEEE International Conference on Computer Systems and Applications, AICCSA-06, UAE, pp. 851–858 (2006)

Chapter 2
Two-Party E-Commerce Protocols

2.1 State-of-the-Art Analysis

In this section, we present the state of the art regarding the notable e-commerce protocols considering scenarios consisting of one customer and one merchant for the exchange of the electronic payment for digital or physical products. The e-commerce protocols for the electronic payment of physical products have a different and more complex architecture than the e-commerce protocols for the electronic payment of digital products, due to the different way in which the product's delivery takes place. Thus, we analyze the proposed solutions for the exchange between electronic payment and digital products and then the proposed solutions for the exchange between electronic payment and physical products.

Until now, many e-commerce protocols for the electronic payment of digital products, which ensure fairness and use an online *TTP*, are proposed, for example, [25, 32]. Because an online *TTP* is involved in each item's exchange, it could be attacked by *denial-of-service* attacks.

The first solution that avoids the disadvantage of using an online *TTP* is proposed by Asokan et al. in [9]. They describe a generic protocol between two parties, for exchanging the digital item which can be electronic payment for a digital product, digital signatures, or data, in which *TTP* intervenes only when a dispute arises between parties. We consider the scenario in which a customer pays for a digital product from a merchant. If the customer and merchant agree with the payment value and the product's description, then the customer sends the payment to the merchant, and the merchant sends the digital product to the customer. If the merchant behaves dishonestly and sends to the customer a product that does not correspond with the agreement conditions, then the customer initiates a recovery sub-protocol with *TTP* to reestablish fairness. The protocol ensures weak fairness, because in the recovery sub-protocol, *TTP* issues an affidavit to the customer that he can use in a court of law to obtain fairness. Also, the protocol provides timeliness, non-repudiation, integrity, and confidentiality.

© The Author(s), under exclusive license to Springer Nature Switzerland AG 2022
C. V. Bîrjoveanu, M. Bîrjoveanu, *Secure Multi-Party E-Commerce Protocols*,
SpringerBriefs in Computer Science, https://doi.org/10.1007/978-3-030-99351-1_2

The (optimistic) e-commerce protocols that ensure strong fairness and use an offline *TTP* are proposed later in [3–5, 30, 33]. Ray et al. propose in [30, 33] an e-commerce protocol based on the theory of cross-validation. For each digital product that the merchant sells, *TTP* encrypts and makes it available on the online catalog. If the customer is interested to buy a digital product, then he downloads the encrypted version of it from catalog and sends to the merchant the purchase order and the encrypted payment. The merchant sends his encrypted version of the digital product to the customer. We remark that the encryption key used by the merchant to encrypt the digital product is a *product key* $K_1 \times K_2$ (used in the theory of cross-validation), where K_1 is the encryption key used by *TTP* to encrypt the same digital product. On reception, the customer compares the two encrypted versions of the digital product: the one received from the merchant with the one downloaded from *TTP*. If the comparison is successful, then the customer is ensured that the product he will receive from the merchant is the one ordered. Therefore, the customer sends the payment decryption key to the merchant. After reception of payment, the merchant sends the product decryption key to the customer. In the case in that the merchant sends to the customer an inappropriate decryption key, the customer contacts *TTP* to restore fairness within the protocol. A shortcoming of this protocol is that *TTP* must encrypt each digital product, which is not usual for a *TTP* that is involved only when a party behaves dishonestly. Also, besides strong fairness, the protocol provides timeliness, non-repudiation, integrity, and confidentiality. In [3–5], Alaraj et al. describe e-commerce protocols ensuring strong fairness for scenarios in which a customer pays to a merchant for acquiring a digital product. These protocols use the assumption of the trustworthiness of one party (customer/merchant) and then force the other party (merchant/customer) to be honest. The protocols from [3, 5] consider a trustworthy customer and enforce the merchant to behave honestly, while the protocol from [4] considers a trustworthy merchant and enforces the customer to behave honestly. In [3, 5], the protocol consists of two sub-protocols: *Pre-Exchange* and *Exchange*. The assumption of the trustworthy customer requires that it obtains two certificates in *Pre-Exchange* sub-protocol: a public key certificate issued by *TTP* that authenticates a public key known only by the customer and *TTP*, and a payment certificate issued by the customer's bank that authenticates the payment value for the digital product desired by the customer. After *Pre-Exchange* sub-protocol run, the customer and merchant exchange the payment and the digital product in *Exchange* sub-protocol that consists of three messages. The customer initiates *Exchange* sub-protocol by sending to the merchant the description of the digital product it desires, the two certificates, the encrypted payment, and a key K encrypted with the merchant's public key. The key K will be used in the next step, by the merchant, to encrypt the digital product. On reception, the merchant checks the customer's certificates authenticity, and if is satisfied, it sends to the customer the digital product encrypted with the key K. If the customer is satisfied with the digital product he receives, then it sends the payment decryption key to the merchant. In this way, the merchant is forced to be honest, because it receives the payment only after it sends the correct digital product to the customer. If the customer sends to the merchant an improper payment decryption key, then the merchant obtains the corresponding decryption key from *TTP*. The problem with this protocol is the assumption of customer's honesty. To fulfill this, *TTP* is involved in protocol not only in the case of a dispute, because it issues an authentic public key certificate for the customer. The protocol from [3, 5] guarantees strong fairness, non-repudiation, integrity, and confidentiality.

Next, we will discuss the state of the art related to the e-commerce protocols used to exchange a digital product for an electronic payment that provide fairness and the customer's privacy. In [31], an e-commerce protocol that uses an offline *TTP* and ensures strong fairness and customer's privacy is proposed, based on the theory of cross-validation from [30] and having many similarities with this. The privacy of the customer in the payment phase is obtained by using a group signature scheme as in [12], on behalf of banks. So, the payment from the customer to the merchant is performed by a payment token signed by the customer's bank using a private key shared by all banks. Therefore, when the signed payment token is received by the merchant's bank, it verifies that the payment token is signed by a valid bank from group, but without knowing the signer bank.

Optimistic e-commerce protocols for buying digital products have been proposed in [22, 23, 33, 43], ensuring fairness and the customer's privacy by using an anonymous electronic cash system based on blind digital signatures from [15]. The e-commerce protocol proposed by Ray et al. in [33] obtains the customer's privacy by integrating in the fair exchange protocol from [30], a payment system based on electronic cash, using a different pseudo-identity for the customer in any subtransaction, and considering a session public/private key pair in any subtransaction. In [43], Zhang et al. describe a protocol used for exchanging digital documents between two parties that provides strong fairness and tries to guarantee the privacy of the two parties. The protocol can be used in a scenario in which one of the parties is a customer who exchanges a payment for a digital product from a merchant. The authors claim that to obtain the customer's privacy, the communication between parties is performed using *Mix-Nets* from [14]. Moreover, to realize payment, an electronic cash system is assumed to be used, but actually it is not integrated in protocol. The authors make also the assumption that the customer/merchant knows the public key of the merchant/customer. The protocol consists of *Document Exchange* sub-protocol and *Off-line Key Recovery* sub-protocol. In *Document Exchange* sub-protocol, the customer sends to the merchant the payment encrypted with a symmetric key K_C and an item KrC encrypted with the merchant's public key that will be used later by the merchant to obtain the payment decryption key K_C. The merchant responds to the customer by sending the digital product encrypted with a symmetric key K_M and an item KrM encrypted with the customer's public key that will be used later by the customer to obtain K_M. Also, the merchant computes and sends to the customer a commitment Co_M whose goal is to ensure the customer that, in case of a dispute, it will get K_M from *TTP*. After the customer successfully verifies the commitment Co_M, then it sends to the merchant a random number r_C. Because KrC is computed depending on K_C and r_C, the merchant uses r_C to get K_C from KrC and further uses K_C to decrypt the payment. Once the merchant obtains payment, it sends to the customer a random number r_M that the customer uses to get K_M from KrM (KrM is computed depending on K_M and r_M) and further to decrypt the digital product. If the customer sends the correct r_C to the merchant, but it receives an improper r_M from the merchant, then it recovers r_M by initiating *Off-line Key Recovery* sub-protocol with *TTP*. For this, the customer sends the correct r_C and Co_M to *TTP*, which can extract r_M from Co_M. *TTP* sends r_M to the customer which can get K_M to decrypt the digital product, assuring strong fairness. Lin et al. [23] describe an e-commerce protocol based on the protocol proposed in [43]. The protocol ensures strong fairness and customer's privacy. The authors obtain the customer's privacy by considering the anonymous communication channels and integrating an electronic cash system based on the partially blind signature scheme from [13].

In [25], Mars et al. propose a solution for buying digital products with the goal of guaranteeing strong fairness and customer's privacy. The solution is based on the fact that both the customer and the merchant can anonymously buy a clone-resistant *Commercial Hardware Token* (*CHT*) they will use in an e-commerce subtransaction. A *CHT* has embedded a *Secret Unknown Cipher* (*SUC*) unit that creates an unpredictable cipher based on a true random generator number, such that the cipher is not known to anyone. The protocol uses an online *TTP* to ensure fairness. The e-commerce protocol consists of two sub-protocols: *CHT Setup* and *Fair Exchange*. In *CHT Setup* sub-protocol, for each *CHT* obtained from the manufacturer, *TTP* generates a set of keys K_i and uses *SUC* from *CHT* to get the encrypted version Y_i of K_i. TTP stores the plaintext/ciphertext pairs (K_i, Y_i) corresponding to each *CHT*, which will be used in *Fair Exchange* sub-protocol to identify *CHT*. After this step, the customer and the merchant can buy a *CHT*, both being identified in *Fair Exchange* sub-protocol by the corresponding *CHT* serial number. In *Fair Exchange* sub-protocol, the customer uses its *CHT* to anonymously order the digital product from the merchant. In response, the merchant requests *TTP* a number Y_i. After the merchant receives Y_i from *TTP*, it can decrypt Y_i using *SUC* from its *CHT* and gets the corresponding K_i. The merchant provides anonymously to the customer the digital product encrypted with K_i, known only by the merchant and *TTP*. On reception, the customer sends to the merchant the payment encrypted with a key which is shared between the customer and *TTP* in *CHT Setup* sub-protocol. The customer confirms to *TTP* that it sent the encrypted payment and it received the encrypted product. Also, the merchant confirms to *TTP* that it sent the encrypted product and it received the encrypted payment. As a result of successfully checking the confirmations, *TTP* provides the product decryption key to the customer and the payment decryption key to the merchant. A shortcoming of this solution is the fact that the authors claim that the payment is performed by a trusted coins generator, but this process is not detailed. Also, *TTP* needs to store many keys for each *CHT* that can become expensive.

Table 2.1 provides a comparative analysis of the security requirements obtained by the notable e-commerce protocols for buying digital products. The notation Yes* is used for the cases in which a protocol guarantees a security requirement, but only in some unusual conditions or assumptions, or using some mechanisms that are necessary to obtain the requirement, but these are not detailed/embedded in

Table 2.1 Comparative analysis of e-commerce protocols for buying digital products

Protocols	Zhang et al. [43]	Ray et al. [33]	Lin et al. [23]	Alaraj et al. [3, 5]	Mars et al. [25]
Effectiveness	Yes	Yes*	Yes	Yes*	No
Strong Fairness	Yes	Yes	Yes	Yes	Yes
Timeliness	No	Yes	Yes	No	No
Non-repudiation	Yes*	Yes	Yes	Yes	Yes
Integrity	Yes	Yes	Yes	Yes	Yes
Confidentiality	Yes	Yes	Yes	Yes	Yes
Customer's Privacy	Yes*	Yes	Yes	No	Yes*

protocol. As shown in Table 2.1, effectiveness is not provided by Mars et al.'s protocol because it is based on a *TTP* involved in each subtransaction. The solution of Ray et al. [33] requires *TTP* to encrypt each digital product, although this task is unusual for a *TTP* that must solve only dispute cases. Also, another shortcoming of Ray et al.'s protocol is that each product must be encrypted (and sent) twice: by *TTP* and merchant. This leads to supplementary storage and the need for more secure management on *TTP*'s side. *TTP*'s involvement in the solution proposed by Alaray et al. [3, 5] is not usual for a protocol with the goal to ensure effectiveness, because *TTP* must issue authentic public key certificates for customers. The solutions of Zhang et al. and Lin et al. provide effectiveness, each product being encrypted only by the merchant, without adding more tasks to *TTP*. All solutions presented in Table 2.1 provide strong fairness, integrity, and confidentiality. Timeliness is ensured only by Ray et al. and Lin et al. protocols; the other protocols do not take into consideration this requirement. Non-repudiation for the customer is required only in the protocol's steps in which the customer's privacy is not required. Zhang et al.'s protocol assumes that each party knows the other's party public key, but the authors do not provide details about how these keys become known. So, if non-repudiation is satisfied, then the question is how is the customer's privacy obtained? If the merchant knows the customer's public key from a digital certificate issued by a certificate authority, then the certificate can reveal customer's identification information to the merchant. Customer's privacy in Mars et al.'s protocol depends on the way in which the payment is performed, more exactly how the customer can anonymously buy digital coins. This mechanism is not embedded in the protocol. Also, usage of *CHTs* adds nevertheless the cost issues, compared to the other discussed solutions.

The first e-commerce protocol which ensures strong fairness for the exchange between the electronic payment and physical products is proposed by Zhang et al. [44]. The merchant responds with a corresponding invoice after the customer's request to buy a physical product. If the customer decides to pay, then it will encrypt the payment twice using the theory of cross-validation from [30]. The first encrypted payment is sent to the merchant and the other to the customer's bank that forwards it to the merchant's bank. The merchant downloads the encrypted payment from his bank and compares it with the encrypted payment received from the customer. If the result is successful, then it is ensured that the payment received from the customer is valid. Further, the merchant sends the product to a delivery cabinet from where the customer takes it. As a result of successful reception, the customer sends the payment decryption key to the merchant. To restore fairness in case of a dispute, the protocol uses the customer's bank as online *TTP*. A shortcoming of this protocol is the need for the customer to encrypt the payment twice. The authors claim that the protocol ensures anonymity of the customer and merchant against any possible coalition between parties, assuming that the communication channels ensure the anonymity of the communicating parties. But the identity of the merchant's bank is included in the invoice which the customer receives, so the customer and the merchant's bank can form a coalition to obtain information about the merchant's identity. Also, the customer's anonymity is not guaranteed because the coalition of the merchant, the merchant's bank, and the customer's bank obtains information about the customer's identity.

Alaraj [2] proposes a solution for buying physical products that is very similar to the solution proposed in [5] for buying digital products. Reasoning in the same way as in [5], the authors consider in [2] a *TTP* that issues a certificate for a public key shared by the customer and *TTP*. This is unusual for an offline *TTP* as the authors claim to use. After the merchant checks the encrypted payment received from the customer, it sends the physical product to a delivery agent that provides the product to the customer. The protocol assures strong fairness but does not ensure effectiveness. Timeliness requirement is obtained using an assumption too strong, namely, that all communication channels used in protocol are resilient.

Djuric et al. [19] propose a *Fair Exchange Internet Payment System* (*FEIPS*) protocol for the electronic payment of physical products. For making electronic payments between the customer and merchant, the payment gateway and the customer's bank are also involved in protocol.

FEIPS is composed of three sub-protocols: *Setup*, *Exchange*, and *Resolution*. All messages in protocol are hybrid encrypted to protect the transmitted information and also to ensure an efficient encryption technique. Hybrid encryption $\{m\}_{PkA}$ of the message m with the public key PkA means $\{m\}_K$, $\{K\}_{PkA}$: the message m is encrypted with an AES session symmetric key K [27], and K is encrypted using PkA. In a protocol's session, two parties will use the same session symmetric key K to hybrid encrypt all the messages they exchange. The protocol is assuming that the customer is equipped with a software named payment Web segment. The *Setup* sub-protocol is used to exchange between the customer and merchant two information necessary in the next messages to identify the customer, respectively, the current protocol's session. Thus, the payment Web segment generates a session public/private key pair for the customer and sends the customer's public key to the merchant, which in turn responds with a random number that will be used to uniquely identify the protocol's session. The *Exchange* sub-protocol performs the exchange of electronic payment for digital receipt between the customer and merchant. For this, the payment Web segment builds a payment message that contains the credit card information of the customer and a challenge code, protects them by hybrid encryption with the payment gateway's public key, and sends it together with the purchase order to the merchant. If the purchase order received by the merchant satisfies him, then he sends the payment message to the payment gateway, which in turn checks if the customer is authorized to use the credit card by checking the credit card information and the challenge code. As a result of successful customer's authorization, the payment gateway requires the customer's bank to make the payment by sending the payment message to it. On successful verification of the customer's account balance, the bank makes the payment, digitally signs an electronic receipt, and sends it to the payment gateway. Otherwise, if the customer's account balance is not enough, the bank digitally signs an aborted response and sends it to the payment gateway. In [19], the communication between the payment gateway and customer's bank is taken into consideration for protocol execution, but the message flow exchanged between them is not described in the protocol's steps. The payment gateway forwards the corresponding digital receipt or aborted response to the merchant, which in turn sends it to the customer. Because the customer receives the corresponding digital receipt only after he sends the payment for the product to the merchant, an unfair situation may occur: the merchant receives the payment from the customer, but he behaves dishonestly and does not send the digital receipt to the customer. For solving this situation, the customer initiates the *Resolution* sub-protocol by sending to the payment gateway a request for the corresponding digital receipt or the aborted response. The payment gateway finds in its database the digital receipt with respect to the current transaction and provides it to the customer. Using the AVISPA tool [39], the authors have proved in [19] that the *FEIPS* protocol ensures strong fairness regarding the exchange of electronic payment for digital receipt, non-repudiation, integrity, and confidentiality. Also, *FEIPS* provides effectiveness and timeliness.

In Sect. 2.2, we will describe the *Subtransaction Protocol* (*SP*), used when a customer buys a physical product from a merchant, which is an extension of the protocol with the same name from [11].

Solutions for obtaining the customer's privacy in the scenario of acquiring physical products have been proposed in [1, 6, 8, 10]. In [1], Aimeur et al. describe a system for physical products delivery based on an *Anonymous Delivery Center* (*ADC*) composed by a set of delivery agents. The customer informs the merchant about the chosen delivery agents and about the mixing message (based on *Mix-Nets* [14]) indicating the route of the physical product. The merchant deposits the product labeled with the mixing message at *ADC*. The product is passed through a mixing mechanism based on [14] using a horizontal rotary surface, in which each delivery agent of *ADC* takes the product and tries to decrypt the mixing message to prepare a corresponding mixing message for the next delivery agent. If the mixing message decryption cannot be successfully performed, the product is placed without modifications on the surface. This mechanism continues until the product reaches the last delivery agent that delivers it to the customer. Considering *ADC* with these functionalities for obtaining customer's privacy is impractical because each delivery agent must decrypt the mixing message whether or not it is on the route chosen by the customer. Also, the authors do not describe how the payment is performed and/or how fairness is guaranteed. In the protocol proposed by Androulaki et al. [8], the customer uses a pseudonym to get a blind credential (by using the group blind digital signatures) from the merchant. The customer uses this credential with the delivery agents to choose the delivery route of the product. After labeling the product according to the route chosen by the customer, its delivery is based on union routing from *Tor* anonymous communication network, ensuring customer's privacy. The problem with this protocol is that fairness is ensured only between delivery agents for the exchange between product's delivery and payment. No solution is provided for the scenario in which the customer receives a product that does not meet compliance requirements. Taking into consideration, many delivery agents makes the whole system difficult. Thus, we consider this protocol quite complicated to be used in practice.

AlTawy et al. [6] and Wang et al. [40] use systems based on *Ethereum blockchain* [20, 41] and smart contracts to deliver physical products. The blockchain is a decentralized structure that consists of linked blocks which contain transactions. The smart contracts were introduced in [37] to facilitate the correct application of the conditions agreed by the contracting parties. In Ethereum, the smart contracts are executed on the network nodes and are applied using *proof-of-work* consensus protocol [21]. Smart contracts behave autonomously and cannot be tampered with, which makes the payment transactions implemented through them to ensure fairness. The system proposed in [6] uses multiple delivery agents to deliver physical products. To obtain the customer's privacy, the customer chooses a different pseudonym in each transaction, and the physical products delivery on the route chosen by him is based on union routing and Crowds [34]. This allows the customer to dynamically decide which delivery agent to pick up the product from. A drawback of this protocol is that it does not guarantee a satisfactory level of fairness, as the customer may receive a counterfeit product while paying for another product. The solution from [40] uses a delivery agent which checks the product's conformity before delivering it. If the customer receives an unsatisfactory product, a return mechanism for the product is proposed. The disadvantages of this solution are the lack of the customer's privacy and the guarantee of only weak fairness by considering a trusted party to solve the possible disputes outside the chain.

Next, we will take a look of some methods used in practice to deliver physical products. *Amazon Locker* [7] can be used when buying products on Amazon. To use this feature, the customers simply add an Amazon Locker to their Amazon address book and select the location as the shipping address during checkout. Once a package is ready for pickup, customers receive an email with a unique six-digit code that they'll use to remove the package from the designated slot. The customer's identity is not completely hidden, because the locker location is stored in the customer's Amazon account. *Private Box* [29] is a virtual address provider which offers to their customer services as PO box addresses, street addresses, and global mail forwarding. At the customer's registration, a valid ID is required. Once the customer buys a product, it can be delivered to private box PO box, and the customer can choose to forward this anywhere in the world. In *Ship Anon* [36], the customer is required to create an account using a nickname, valid email address, and ID. After this, the customer chooses a locker for which the customer pays a fee. When the customer orders the product online, it will be delivered to the locker and can be picked up using a code. For both *Private Box* and *Ship Anon*, the service provider knows the real identity of the customer.

In Sect. 2.3, we describe a *Protocol including Physical Product Delivery that provides the Customer's Privacy* (*PPPDCP*) that improves the protocol proposed in [10].

2.2   Subtransaction Protocol

The participants in *SP* are the customer, the merchant, the payment gateway, and the customer bank. *SP* is composed from two sub-protocols: *Exchange* and *Resolution*.

Unlike *FEIPS* from [19], the subtransaction's identifier in *SP* is generated by the customer, which enables us to eliminate the *Setup* sub-protocol from [19]. Compared with the protocol from [11], this extension includes also the message flow between the payment gateway and the customer bank.

The notations used in the description of *Subtransaction Protocol* and message structures are provided in Table 2.2. The hybrid encryption has the same meaning as in [19]. The communication channels between PG and any other party are considered resilient, and the other communication channels are unreliable. The

Table 2.2 Notations used in *SP* description

Notation	Interpretation
C,M,PG,CB	Identity of Customer, Merchant, Payment Gateway, Customer Bank
$A \rightarrow B : m$	A sends the message m to B
PkA	RSA public key of the party A
K	AES session symmetric key
$\{m\}_{PkA}$	Hybrid encryption of the message m with PkA: $\{m\}_K$, $\{K\}_{PkA}$
$h(m)$	Digest of m obtained by applying of a hash function h [28]
$SigA(m)$	RSA digital signature [35] of A on $h(m)$
PO	Purchase Order: $\{PM, OI\}_{PkM}$
PM	Payment Message: $\{PI, SigC(PI)\}_{PkPG}$
PI	Payment Information: $C, Cn, Otp, Id, Am, PkC, M$
OI	Order Information: $C, M, Pid, Id, Am, PkC, SigC(C, M, Pid, Id, Am, PkC)$
PR	Payment Request: $\{PM, M_{ac}, SigM(Id, C, M, PkC, Am, M_{ac})\}_{PkPG}$
PAR	Payment Authorization Request: $\{PI, M_{ac}, SigPG(PI, M_{ac})\}_{PkCB}$
PA	Payment Acknowledgment: $Resp, C, M, Id, SigCB(Resp, C, M, Id, Am)$
PE	Payment Evidence: $Resp, C, M, Id, SigPG(Resp, C, M, Id, Am)$
PER	Payment Evidence Request: $\{C, M, Id, Am, SigC(Id, Am)\}_{PkPG}$

Fig. 2.1 *SP* message flow

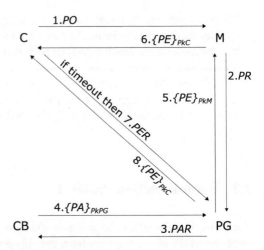

customer downloads automatically a payment Web segment software, when he chooses the product he wants to buy. The payment Web segment performs the customer's side protocol steps, being a software digitally signed by payment gateway which is *TTP*. Thus, the protocol ensures that the payment Web segment cannot be fraudulently modified by the customer or merchant so that they can gain certain benefits, increasing the mutual trust level. When the customer performs some action, in fact we mean that the payment Web segment performs the action on customer's behalf. We consider that the payment Web segment has the digital certificates for the public keys of each merchant and payment gateway. Also, we consider that only payment gateway has the authentic public key certificate of the customer bank and the merchant and payment gateway have each other's digital certificates for their public keys.

In what follows, we will present the *Exchange* and *Resolution* sub-protocol messages that are graphically represented in Fig. 2.1.

2.2.1   Exchange Sub-protocol

The user is browsing through the online catalog where the merchants post their products. When the user finds in the online catalog the product he wants to buy, he initiates *Exchange* sub-protocol by clicking a "submit" button available on the online catalog. This action of the user corresponds to the customer C downloading the payment Web segment. The payment Web segment sends to the merchant M the purchase order PO consisting of two components, a payment message PM and an order information message OI, both of them hybrid encrypted with M's public key PkM.

Message 1: $C \rightarrow M : PO$

The customer C builds PM by encrypting with PG's public key of the payment information PI and his signature on PI.

As we can see in Table 2.2, PI contains the following information:

- Data provided by the user: his identity C, card number Cn, and a one-time password Otp. The customer bank CB generates a one-time password Otp as a fresh number with a minimum length of six digits and provides it to the user via SMS. The role of Otp is to provide a supplementary level of authenticity when it is presented by the customer.
- A fresh random number Id generated by the customer that will be used as a unique identifier of the subtransaction.
- The amount Am that will be paid by the customer, the customer's public key PkC generated by payment Web segment, and the merchant's identity M.

The order information OI consists of the identity of the customer C, the merchant M, the product's identifier Pid, the subtransaction identifier Id, the amount Am, the customer's public key PkC, and the customer's signature on all these information.

When M receives message 1, he decrypts it and checks the customer signature and the information from OI. After merchant's agreement with OI, he sends to PG a payment request message PR to obtain the payment from the customer.

Message 2: $M \rightarrow PG : PR$

In the payment request message, M includes the payment message PM, his account information M_{ac} at his bank, and his signature on Id and Am as a confirmation of his agreement with C. After PG receives the payment request from M, he decrypts it and checks C's signature on PI and M's signature. Successful verification of signatures ensures PG of the agreement between C and M on Id and Am. To avoid any possible replay attack from merchants with dishonest behavior, PG checks also if the subtransaction identifier Id is fresh. If some check is not successfully passed, then PG aborts the subtransaction by sending to M an $ABORT$ response. If all checks are successful, PG sends to the customer bank a payment authorization request PAR in message 3.

Message 3: $PG \rightarrow CB : PAR$

PG builds PAR by signing the payment information PI and the merchant's account information M_{ac} and encrypting it with CB's public key $PkCB$. On the reception of message 3, CB decrypts it and verifies PG's signature on PI and M_{ac}. CB authenticates C on the payment information by checking validity of the pair (Cn, Otp). If the pair (Cn, Otp) is valid, then the customer proves the knowledge of the card number Cn and also the possession of the device for Otp reception in a two-factor authentication. Otherwise, if the pair (Cn, Otp) is not valid, then CB provides an $ABORT$ response $(Resp = ABORT)$ to PG.

If the customer's authentication is successful, then CB authorizes C to use the card by verifying the C's account balance. If C's account balance is sufficient, then CB performs the money transfer in M's account providing a payment acknowledgment PA with $Resp = YES$ to PG in message 4. If C's account balance is not sufficient, then CB provides an $ABORT$ response to PG in message 4.

Message 4: $CB \rightarrow PG : \{PA\}_{PkPG}$

Depending on the response PG receives in message 4, it sends the payment evidence PE to M in message 5. So, if PG receives PA from CB, then PE contains the corresponding YES response. Otherwise, if PG receives an $ABORT$ response from CB, then PE contains the corresponding $ABORT$ response. To keep a record of the subtransaction details, PG stores messages 2, 4, and 5 in its databases.

Message 5: $PG \rightarrow M : \{PE\}_{PkM}$

The merchant M decrypts the payment evidence PE received from PG, encrypts it with PkC, and sends it to C, in message 6.

Message 6: $M \rightarrow C : \{PE\}_{PkC}$

C decrypts message 6 and checks the authenticity of PE by checking PG's signature. If the payment evidence PE contains Id and Am, then this ensures C of payment evidence freshness and that it corresponds to the current subtransaction. A successful payment evidence PE (with $Resp = YES$) provides to C the guarantee that the subtransaction successfully finished. An aborted payment evidence PE (with $Resp = ABORT$) informs C that the subtransaction is aborted.

2.2.2   Resolution Sub-protocol

In *Exchange* sub-protocol, a scenario in which fairness is not ensured can appear. In this scenario, the customer is disadvantaged: C pays to M, but he does not receive the corresponding payment evidence PE from M. To solve this problem, a timeout interval t (e.g., in the order of seconds or minutes) is defined, in which C waits the corresponding PE in message 6 from M. If C does not receive message 6 from M and t expires, then C initiates the resolution sub-protocol by sending a payment evidence request PER to PG to receive the payment evidence corresponding to the current subtransaction.

Message 7: $C \rightarrow PG : PER$

After receiving message 7, PG decrypts it, checks the customer's signature authenticity, and searches in its database a payment evidence corresponding to the entry C, M, Id, $Amount$. If PG finds in its database such a payment evidence, then he sends it to C in message 8. If PG does not find a corresponding payment evidence for the entry above, then PG generates an aborted payment evidence for this entry and sends it to C in message 8. Messages 7 and 8 from are also stored by PG in its database.

Message 8: $PG \rightarrow C : \{PE\}_{PkC}$

SP Security Discussion

SP ensures the following security requirements: effectiveness, strong fairness, timeliness, non-repudiation, integrity, and confidentiality. Effectiveness is provided in *SP* because if every party involved in protocol behaves honestly, then the merchant receives the payment from the customer, and the customer receives the corresponding payment evidence from the merchant, and this takes place without the intervention of *TTP*. Strong fairness, non-repudiation, integrity, and confidentiality are satisfied by *SP*, all these requirements being formally proved in [11] using AVISPA. To ensure timeliness, *SP* uses the timeout interval t (for the case in which the customer does not receive the corresponding payment evidence) and also the resilient communication channels between payment gateway and any other party.

2.3 Protocol with Physical Product Delivery Providing Customer's Privacy

PPPDCP eliminates the disadvantage of online *TTP* usage of the solution from [10], using instead an offline *TTP* and still providing customer's privacy and fair exchange between electronic payment and physical product reception. To achieve this result, we make some improvements to the solution from [10], as follows:

- In *PPPDCP*, the customer performs payment to the merchant first, and then the merchant delivers the physical product. In [10], the customer sends the encrypted payment to the merchant, then the product delivery is performed, and finally the customer makes the payment to the merchant by sending it a corresponding decryption key of the encrypted payment.
- To maintain the customer's privacy in the payment phase, we use the *blind digital signature* proposed in [16], while in [10], the *group blind digital signature* proposed in [24] is used. However, the blind digital signature we consider is much more efficient compared to the group blind digital signature used in [10].
- *PPPDCP* considers a delivery cabinet under the merchant's control that is closer to the real-world transactions involving physical products delivery (e.g., Amazon Locker). The protocol from [10] considers the delivery cabinet as a standalone entity. Our delivery system has some similarities with the Amazon Locker, meaning that the customer can choose a box (locker) where the product is to be delivered. But in our protocol, the box's location is not associated in any manner with the customer's account. Also, like in Amazon Locker, the customer does not pay a fee for using the box.

PPPDCP has the following participants: the customer and his bank, the merchant and his bank, the delivery agent, the destination cabinet, and the trusted third party. Our *PPPDCP* uses a trusted third party agreed by all other participants in the protocol that intervenes only in the case of a dispute between participants to restore fairness. Table 2.3 shows the notations used in the *PPPDCP*'s description and the structure of its messages. We use in *PPPDCP* the same notation for hybrid encryption as in the *Subtransaction Protocol*'s description from Sect. 2.2.

Table 2.3 Notations used in *PPPDCP* description

Notation	Interpretation
C, M, CB, MB	Identity of Customer, Merchant, Customer's Bank, Merchant's Bank
DA, DC, TTP	Delivery Agent, Destination Cabinet, Trusted Third Party
C'	Pseudo identity of the Customer
$A - \to B : m$	A sends the message m to B using *Tor*
$RBSC$	Request for Blind Signature on Coin: $\{PI, SigC(PI)\}_{PkCB}$
PI	Payment Information: C, Cn, Otp, Am, M, Bl
PO	Purchase Order: $\{OI, SigC'(OI)\}_{PkM}$
OI	Order Information: $C', M, Pid, Id, Dgc, SigCB(Dgc), DC_{ad}, PkC', CB$
PR	Payment Request:
	$\{Dgc, SigCB(Dgc), SigM(Dgc, SigCB(Dgc)), Id, C', CB, M, M_{ac}\}_{PkMB}$
AR	Abort Request: $\{ABORT, Dgc, SigCB(Dgc), SigM(Dgc, SigCB(Dgc)),$
	$Id, C', CB, M\}_{PkMB}$
PE	Payment Evidence: $Resp, C', M, Id, SigMB(Resp, C', M, Id, Am)$
DO	Delivery Order: $\{DI, SigM(DI)\}_{PkDA}$
DI	Delivery Information: $Id, Pid, Pw_M, M, DA, DC_{ad}$
PCA	Product Collection Acknowledgment: $Id, SigDA(Id, Pid, M, DA, DC_{ad})$
PRA	Product Reception Acknowledgment: $Id, SigDC(Id, Pid, M, DA, DC_{ad})$

The customer and merchant communicate using *Tor* anonymous communication network [18] that maintains the customer's privacy. All other participants communicate using resilient channels. The resilient communication channels between C/M and his bank CB/MB are implemented by the corresponding bank CB/MB (each bank provides a high level of trust). The communication channels between M and DA, DA and DC, and $C(C')$ and DC are considered resilient because in each of the above communication pairs at least one participant must be physically there.

We consider that only the customer's bank CB has the authentic public key certificate of the customer C, and any other participant has the digital certificates for the authentic public keys of other participants, necessary to verify the digital signatures included in the messages he receives.

The customer and merchant banks CB and MB share a commit-buffer in that the transaction value is stored until the transaction is completed successfully or aborted. Also, to prevent double spending or double canceling of the digital coins used in protocol, the banks share a list of currently used digital coins. Each record in the list consists of the digital coin and a corresponding *spent* flag describing the coin's state. The *spent* flag can have two values, each with the following meaning:

- *spent* = 1 means that the coin has already been spent; this value of the *spent* flag can be modified only to the value 0 if a request for canceling for this digital coin appears.
- *spent* = 0 means that the coin has already been canceled; this value of the *spent* flag cannot be modified.

We consider the existence of a destination cabinet DC, which is a box system like Amazon Lockers, where each box is accessible via a password generated by M. When DC is enrolled in the system, a Delivery Segment software is installed on it. The Delivery Segment is a software digitally signed by TTP, and his role is to perform DC's side protocol steps. So, the protocol ensures that the Delivery Segment software cannot be broken by a dishonest merchant so that it can obtain some advantages against the other participants. DC have the ability to digitally sign messages, to verify digital signatures on messages, and to check if the password entered by C is the same with the one set by the delivery agent DA on the corresponding box. Thus, using DC allows hiding the true identity of the customer and preserving its privacy.

A video camera is mounted at DC to record the moment when C collects the product and checks if it is the ordered one. If C is not satisfied with the collected product, then DC allows it, by pushing a "reject button," to send to TTP the encrypted recording from the time of product's verification. Otherwise, if C agrees with the collected product, then the recording is automatically deleted.

The Onion Router

The Onion Router (Tor) [18] is the most popular anonymous communication network used by continuously increasing number of peoples. *Tor* provides a high privacy level for users by sending the messages to their recipients using a set of volunteers *union routers (ORs)*. Currently, *Tor* is composed of over 6000 ORs [38]. Information about ORs are distributed on *directory servers*. The user's software downloads the signed *Tor* network's status and the list of ORs from the configured directory servers. The *Tor* functionality is based on creating secure communication circuits through which messages (which have several levels of encryption applied) are sent between the user's software as initiator I of the stream and the receiver R, in order to hide the full path that messages travel from source to destination.

Figure 2.2 shows the *Tor*'s functionality when the initiator I wants to exchange messages with a receiver R with the protection of its privacy. I creates a circuit by randomly choosing of three union routers OR_1, OR_2, and OR_3 (*Tor* uses minimum three ORs in a circuit), over which its communication is relayed, until it reaches the final destination R. I starts the creation of a new circuit by sending to the first chosen OR_1 a new random circuit identifier C_1 and the encryption with RSA OR_1's public key $PkOR_1$ of his data g^{x_1} necessary in the ephemeral Diffie-Hellman key exchange [17]. OR_1 responds to I by sending his data g^{y_1}, and a digest of the new AES session key $K_1 = g^{x_1y_1}$, to confirm to I the knowledge of K_1. After establishing the key K_1, I and OR_1 will use it to encrypt the messages exchanged between them. I extends the circuit established with OR_1, by sending it a request encrypted with K_1. The request contains the address of the next union router OR_2 and his data g^{x_2} encrypted with $PkOR_2$. OR_1 generates a new circuit identifier C_2 and forwards $\{g^{x_2}\}_{PkOR_2}$ to OR_2. OR_2 responds to OR_1 in the same manner as OR_1 responds to the first message of I. In turn, OR_1 sends to I the data g^{y_2} received from OR_2, encrypted with their established key K_1. So, I and OR_2 establish the new session key $K_2 = g^{x_2y_2}$, OR_2 becoming the second onion router from the path.

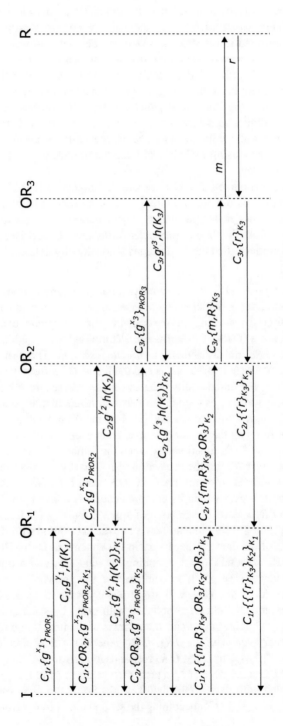

Fig. 2.2 I sends the message m to R, and R responds with the message r to I through three ORs of *Tor* network

In the same manner, I extends the circuit with a new onion router OR_3 by sending a corresponding request to the last onion router from circuit OR_2. As a result, I creates a circuit establishing a new session key with each OR from the circuit. In this way, no OR can trace the messages that pass through it. Each OR in the created circuit knows only OR from which it receives data and OR to which it sends data, without being able to know the entire route of a data and to make a link between I and R.

After building the circuit, I can send messages to R through the onion routers OR_1, OR_2, and OR_3 from circuit. I encapsulates the message m he wants to send to R by iterative encryption of it with the session keys established with each OR from circuit, in the reverse order (from farthest to closest), as follows: $\{\{\{m, R\}_{K_3}, OR_3\}_{K_2}, OR_2\}_{K_1}$. I sends this message to the first onion router OR_1, which removes an encryption level by decrypting it with K_1 and sends the result $\{\{\{m, R\}_{K_3}, OR_3\}_{K_2}, OR_2\}_{K_1}$ to the next onion router OR_2. Similarly, after decryption of $\{\{\{m, R\}_{K_3}, OR_3\}_{K_2}$ with K_2, OR_2 sends the result $\{\{m, R\}_{K_3}$ to OR_3, which in turn decrypts it with K_3 and sends m to R.

When R responds with a message r to the initiator, then r is sent through the same ORs from circuit, but in the reverse order: OR_3, OR_2, and OR_1. Each OR adds an encryption level using his session key established with I and sends the result to the next OR from the circuit. Thus, R sends r to OR_3 that sends C_3, $\{r\}_{K_3}$ to OR_2, which in turn sends C_2, $\{\{r\}_{K_3}\}_{K_2}$ to OR_1, which in turn sends C_1, $\{\{\{r\}_{K_3}\}_{K_2}\}_{K_1}$ to I. Finally, only I can get r by iterative decryption of the message received from OR_1 using the session keys K_1, K_2, and K_3, in this order.

Tor is not intended to provide protection against end-to-end correlation attacks. In such attacks, if the attacker can monitor the traffic coming out from I and the one that reaches R, then he can infer that I and R belong to the same circuit. The goal of *Tor* is to protect the privacy of I against an attacker that can observe and control a part of the network, but not the entire network. Many research articles in the literature present scenarios of attack on *Tor*. One of the most cited articles that presents an attack on *Tor* is [26]. The attack from [26] is a traffic-analysis attack that allows an attacker to deduce which ORs relays the stream, assuming that the attacker has control on a part of the network. Although some streams can be associated with the same initiator, still the privacy of I is preserved, because the attack cannot determine that I is connected to an OR. We consider that *Tor* provides a high level of privacy offering a good enough balance between the privacy of I, security, and efficiency.

Another solution that also provides a good enough balance between privacy and resilience is proposed in [42]. This solution proposes a hybrid routing mechanism by adding the hop-by-hop routing in *Mix-Nets* proposed in [14].

PPPDCP consists of the *Subtransaction Payment* sub-protocol *SPayment*, the *Subtransaction Delivery* sub-protocol *SDelivery*, and three *Resolution* sub-protocols. *SPayment* and *SDelivery* sub-protocol messages are represented in Fig. 2.3. Below, we describe each sub-protocol of *PPPDCP*.

Fig. 2.3 *SPayment* and
SDelivery sub-protocols
message flow. The physical
collection/placement of the
product is represented by a
dotted arrow

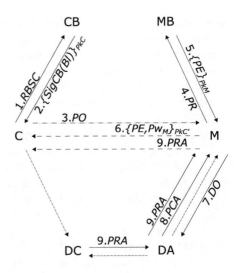

2.3.1   SPayment Sub-protocol

The user is looking for the physical product he is interested in by browsing the
online catalog that makes available the products that merchants want to sell. If the
product sought by the user is made available on catalog by the merchant M, then he
initiates the *SPayment* sub-protocol by activation of a "submit" button available on
the catalog.

Then, the customer C sends to his bank CB a request for buying a digital coin of
a corresponding value which he will use to purchase the product from the merchant
M. For buying a digital coin, we use a blind digital signature on the digital coin,
which in fact is an RSA digital signature on *blinded* version of the digital coin.
The blind digital signatures were introduced in [15] to ensure the payer's privacy
in electronic cash systems. We integrate in *PPPDCP* the blind digital signature
from [16], adapted to allow buying of the digital coins of various values, as follows.
In the first message, C sends to his bank a request for a blind signature on coin
$RBSC$, consisting of the payment information PI and C's signature on it, both
encrypted with the RSA public key $PkCB$ of CB. We consider the RSA public key
$PkCB$ as being the pair (e, N) and the corresponding RSA private key of CB as
being the pair (d, N).

   Message 1: $C \rightarrow CB : RBSC$

   The components $C, Cn, Otp, Am, and M$ of PI have the same meaning as the
components with the same name of the payment information used in *Subtransaction
Protocol* from Sect. 2.2. The sixth component Bl of PI is the blinded version of the
digital coin Dgc generated by C. Bl is generated by C, as follows:

1. C generates a digital coin $Dgc = SnAm$ as a number of 256 bits consisting of a
   unique random serial number Sn of 224 bits and the value Am of Dgc represented
   on the last 32 bits of Dgc.

2. C generates a random number Bf as a random blinding factor for Dgc, such that $gcd(Bf, N) = 1$.
3. C computes $Bl = Bf^e*Dgc \bmod N$.

After the reception of the request $RBSC$ from C, CB decrypts it and checks the customer's signature on PI to ensure the $RBSC$'s authenticity. Then, CB authenticates C by checking the validity of the pair (Cn, Otp). If the pair (Cn, Otp) is not valid, then CB sends to C an aborted payment evidence $Resp, C, M, Id,$ $SigCB(Resp, C, M, Id, Am)$, with $Resp = ABORT$.

After successful customer's authentication, CB authorizes C to use the card by verifying C's account balance. If C's account balance is sufficient compared to the requested coin's value, then CB makes the money transfer from C's account in the commit-buffer. CB cannot obtain Dgc from Bl because it doesn't know the blinding factor Bf. CB responds to C by sending in message 2 his signature on the blinded coin Bl, encrypted with the public key PkC of C. Otherwise, if C's account balance is not sufficient, then CB sends an aborted payment evidence to C.

Message 2: $CB \rightarrow C : \{SigCB(Bl)\}_{PKC}$

CB computes his RSA signature $SigCB(Bl)$ on Bl using his RSA private key (d, N), as follows:

$$SigCB(Bl) = (Bf^e * Dgc \bmod N)^d \bmod N$$
$$= Bf^{ed} * Dgc^d \bmod N = Bf * Dgc^d \bmod N$$

The customer obtains $SigCB(Bl)$ by decrypting message 2. C gets the signature $SigCB(Dgc)$ of CB on the digital coin Dgc by removing the blinding factor Bf from $SigCB(Bl)$, as below:

$$SigCB(Dgc) = Bf^{-1} * SigCB(Bl)$$

After C obtains CB's signature on the digital coin Dgc, he sends the purchase order PO to the merchant M. To hide its real identity, the customer uses Tor anonymous network to communicate with M. In each protocol's session, the customer doesn't use his real identity in the communication with M, but he will use a new session pseudo-identity C' and a new session public key PkC'.

Message 3: $C \dashrightarrow M : PO$

As we can see in Table 2.3, PO is composed of the order information OI and the customer's signature on OI using the session private key corresponding to his session public key PkC'. OI contains the following elements: the pseudo-identity C', the identity of merchant M, the product identifier Pid, the subtransaction identifier Id, the digital coin Dgc, CB's signature on Dgc, the mailing address DC_{ad} of destination cabinet where the customer can collect the product, the session public key PkC' generated by the customer only for usage in this session, and the identity of customer bank CB.

On the reception of message 3, M decrypts PO and uses the public key PkC' to validate the signature of the customer on OI. If M agrees with OI, then he sends a payment request PR to his bank MB for the redemption of the digital coin Dgc received in OI. Otherwise, if M doesn't agree with OI (e.g., the Dgc's value does not correspond to the product's value), then he sends to MB a corresponding abort request AR.

Message 4: $M \rightarrow MB : PR$ or AR

PR contains the digital coin Dgc, signature $SigCB(Dgc)$, signature of M on both of them, pseudo-identity C', identity of CB, identity of merchant M, and M's account information M_{ac} at MB.

If MB receives PR, then he decrypts it, checks CB's signature on Dgc and M's signature on $(Dgc, SigCB(Dgc))$, and searches the coin Dgc in the list of currently used digital coins to check if it has already been used in previous protocol sessions. If the signatures are successfully validated and Dgc is not found in the list, then MB transfers Dgs's value Am from commit-buffer to M_{ac}, adds the coin Dgc to the coin's list, sets the *spent* flag of Dgc to 1, and sends to M a successful payment evidence PE (with $Resp = YES$). Otherwise, if some check is not satisfied, MB sends to M an aborted payment evidence PE.

If MB receives AR, then he performs the same checks as for PR. If the checks are successful, then MB adds the coin Dgc to the coin's list, sets the *spent* flag of Dgc to 0, and sends to M an aborted payment evidence PE (with $Resp = ABORT$).

Message 5: $MB \rightarrow M : \{PE\}_{PkM}$

When M receives PE, he checks the authenticity of PE by checking MB's signature validity. M responds to the customer using *Tor* communication network depending on the success or abortion of PE. So, if M receives an aborted PE, then he forwards it to the customer. If M receives a successful PE, then he generates a random number Pw_M that will be used as an access password for collecting the product from one of the DC's boxes. In this case, M sends to the customer the successful PE and the password Pw_M, both encrypted with session public key PkC'.

Message 6: $M \longrightarrow C : \{PE, Pw_M\}_{PkC'}$

After the reception of message 6, the customer decrypts it and gets PE and the password Pw_M.

2.3.2 SDelivery Sub-protocol

If after *SPayment* sub-protocol's run, M receives a successful payment evidence as a proof of successful reception of payment from the customer, then he sends in message 7 a delivery order DO to the delivery agent DA. We consider without loss of generality that DA is a representative of a delivery company worldwide spread.

Message 7: $M \rightarrow DA : DO$

The order delivery DO contains the delivery information DI and M's signature on DI, both encrypted with the public key $PkDA$ of DA. M includes in DI the following information: the subtransaction identifier Id, the product identifier Pid, the access password Pw_M, and the delivery address DC_{ad} of destination cabinet where the product must be delivered.

DA checks M's signature to verify the authenticity of DI, collects the product P with Pid identifier from M, and sends a product collection acknowledgment PCA to M in message 8.

Message 8: $DA \rightarrow M : PCA$

DA places the product P in one of the DC's boxes at DC_{ad} address, setting Pw_M as the access password to the box that contains P. To confirm the reception of the product P from DA, DC sends to it a product reception acknowledgment PRA which is a signature of DC on the subtransaction's information as shown in Table 2.3.

Message 9: $DC \rightarrow DA : PRA$

PRA is forwarded by DA to M, which in turn forwards it to the customer. When the customer receives the product reception acknowledgment PRA, he collects P from DC using the access password Pw_M. The electronic payment method from M to DA for the delivery service is a usual payment method that does not require privacy (of M or DA), that is why it is not described here. Also, this payment can be realized either after message 8 or 9.

2.3.3 Resolution Sub-protocols

In *PPPDCP*, C pays first to M, and then M delivers the physical product to C. So, there can be three scenarios in which C is in a more disadvantaged position than M:

1. C pays to M in message 3, but he does not receive message 6 that contains PE and Pw_M or receives an abort message from M. This scenario is solved by applying *Resolution 1* sub-protocol.
2. C pays to M and receives a successful PE in message 6 but doesn't receive PRA in message 9. This scenario is solved by applying *Resolution 2* sub-protocol.
3. C pays to M and receives a successful PE and PRA, but he is not satisfied with the product collected from DC_{ad}. This scenario is solved by applying *Resolution 3* sub-protocol.

Resolution 1 Sub-protocol

In the first scenario from above, C waits a timeout interval to receive PE and Pw_M, and if this interval expires without reception of them, then C initiates *Resolution 1* sub-protocol by sending to TTP a request for the evidence's reception.

$$C \longrightarrow TTP : \{OI, SigC'(OI)\}_{PkTTP}$$

TTP verifies the request received from the customer and asks MB for the payment evidence corresponding to OI, as follows:

$$TTP \rightarrow MB : \{OI, SigC'(OI), SigTTP(OI, SigC'(OI))\}_{PkMB}$$

Depending on the existence in MB's database of PE corresponding to OI, the following cases can appear:

1. If MB finds in its database an aborted payment evidence PE corresponding to OI, then this means that the digital coin Dgc from OI has already been used and Dgc is present in the coin's list. In this case, MB sends the aborted PE to TTP, which in turn sends it to the customer.
2. If MB finds in its database a successful PE, then it must be aborted and the corresponding digital coin Dgc canceled (because C has paid for Dgc but he doesn't have the corresponding password Pw_M). Thus, MB aborts PE, updating it as follows:

$$PE1 = PE \text{ and } PE = ABORT, C', M, Id, SigMB(ABORT, C', M, Id, Am, PE1).$$

Also, MB transfers Dgc's value Am from M_{ac} to commit-buffer, sets the *spent* flag of Dgc to 0, and sends the updated aborted PE to TTP and M. After receiving the updated PE, TTP sends to the customer a canceling request that includes PE, as follows:

$$TTP \longrightarrow C : \{T_{TTP}, PE, Cancel, SigTTP(T_{TTP}, Am, Cancel)\}_{PkC'}$$

On the reception of the canceling request from TTP, the customer forwards it to his bank, as below:

$$C \rightarrow CB : \{T_{TTP}, Am, Cancel, C, SigTTP(T_{TTP}, Am, Cancel)\}_{PkCB}$$

CB checks the freshness of the canceling request by verifying the timestamp T_{TTP} of TTP and TTP's signature. If all these checks are successfully passed, CB transfers Am from commit-buffer to customer's account and sends to the customer a corresponding acknowledgment.
3. If MB doesn't find PE in its database, then this means that Dgc was not used, and it must be canceled. Thus, MB generates an aborted payment evidence PE corresponding to OI, adds Dgc with the *spent* flag on 0 in the coin's list, and sends PE to TTP and M. From this step, TTP sends the canceling request to the customer, which in turn contacts his bank to recover the money corresponding to Dgc's value, as in case 2 above.

Resolution 2 Sub-protocol

In the second scenario, C waits a timeout interval to receive PRA, and if this interval expires without reception of it, then C initiates *Resolution 2* sub-protocol by sending to TTP a request that in addition to OI includes the successful PE and the password Pw_M already received from M. This scenario is solved in a similar manner with *Resolution 1* sub-protocol case 2.

Resolution 3 Sub-protocol

In the third scenario, if the customer is not satisfied with the product received in DC's box, then he press the "reject button" from DC that allows him sending to TTP the encrypted recording of the moment in which he collects the physical product. Also, C sends to TTP all the information sent/received to/from M in the current subtransaction: OI, the successful PE, Pw_M, and PRA. From this step, *Resolution 3* sub-protocol continues in the same manner with *Resolution 1* sub-protocol case 2.

2.3.4   Security Analysis

PPPDCP provides effectiveness, strong fairness, timeliness, non-repudiation, integrity, confidentiality, and privacy of customer.

If every party involved in protocol behaves honestly, then the customer receives the physical product from the merchant, and the merchant receives the payment for his product from the customer. In this case, *TTP* is not involved in protocol, so *PPPDCP* ensures effectiveness.

Strong fairness in *PPPDCP* requires that either the customer acquires the physical product from the merchant and the merchant gets payment for the product or none of them obtains nothing. To detail the reasons for that *PPPDCP* provides strong fairness, we consider all scenarios in which C, M, DA, or DC behaves dishonestly. Because C receives the product only after he pays for it, the only scenarios in which he can behave dishonestly are in *SPayment* sub-protocol. If C tries to make double spending of a digital coin, then this is detected by MB in message 4. C's attempt to make double canceling by sending a PO that contains a digital coin that has already been canceled is detected by MB in message 4. Also, if C tries to make double canceling by sending a request directly to CB, then CB detects it in *Resolution 1* sub-protocol, case 2. If C sends a PO that contains a digital coin with an insufficient value, then he cannot obtain any benefit because M sends AR to MB. In this case, MB generates a corresponding aborted payment evidence and sends it to M in message 5.

M can behave dishonestly in *SPayment* or *SDelivery* sub-protocols. In *SPayment* sub-protocol, M can try to make double redemption, but this is detected by MB. Also, in *SPayment* sub-protocol, M can receive payment from the customer, but he doesn't send the corresponding PE and Pw_M to the customer. This scenario corresponds to the scenario 1 presented in Sect. 2.3.3 and is solved by applying *Resolution 1* sub-protocol. M can behave dishonestly in *SDelivery* sub-protocol in the following scenarios: M sends PE and Pw_M but does not send PRA to the customer, or M sends PE, Pw_M, and PRA but does not deliver the physical product according to the specifications of the agreed PO. These scenarios correspond to the scenarios 2 and 3 presented in Sect. 2.3.3 and are solved by applying *Resolution 2* and *3* sub-protocols.

The only scenario in which the delivery agent DA behaves dishonestly is when he collects a physical product from M, but he places another product to DC's box from DC_{ad} address. In this scenario, the customer will not be satisfied with the product delivered to DC, and then he press the "reject button" requiring TTP to abort the corresponding payment evidence and cancel the corresponding digital coin. *Resolution 3* sub-protocol is applied, and therefore, strong fairness between the customer and merchant in *PPPDCP* is preserved.

In *PPPDCP*, DC is owned by M, but its behavior is controlled by a Delivery Segment software digitally signed by TTP. So, no party can corrupt this software for its benefit.

Any participant from *PPPDCP* is ensured that *PPPDCP*'s execution will be finished at a certain finite point of time. This requirement is obtained by using timeout intervals in the scenarios in which the customer does not receive the corresponding messages from M and also by using the resilient communication channels between any other parties (except between customer and merchant). After the protocol finish point, either C acquires the physical product and M gets the payment (in this case, both C and M receive a corresponding successful payment evidence), or C does not acquire the product and M does not obtain the payment (in this case, both C and M receive an aborted payment evidence). Thus, timeliness is ensured in *PPPDCP*.

None of the participants in *PPPDCP* can deny its involvement in *PPPDCP*, because each of them sends his digital signatures in the protocol's messages. Thus, M includes his signature in PR and DO, DA uses his digital signature for PCA generation, and DC signs PRA. *PPPDCP* provides customer's privacy, so C cannot deny its involvement in *PPPDCP* only in buying the digital coin from his bank. As a result, *PPPDCP* provides non-repudiation.

Each message sent in *PPPDCP* includes the sender's digital signature of the hash code of the information sent. Thus, *PPPDCP* ensures the integrity requirement of the exchanged data between parties, any unauthorized modification of the transmitted data being detected at reception by checking the corresponding signature.

PPPDCP provides confidentiality because each message transmitted between parties involved is hybrid encrypted with the public key of the receiver.

The customer's privacy is a challenging issue in the e-commerce protocols, because in an e-commerce transaction, the customer may be interested not to reveal to the merchant his sensitive data such as his real identity, credit card number, or bank account number. M can collect these data and link them with the transactions in which the customer is involved. This allows M to build a commercial profile for the customer and use it for business reasons. Thus, M can apply commercial discrimination based on the customer's commercial profile data: bought products, nationality, gender, and affiliation. Customer's privacy is guaranteed in *PPPDCP* if the customer remains anonymous and if the link between his real identity and the transactions in which he is involved cannot be made by any of the other *PPPDCP*'s participants and by any coalition between them (that can include other entities not involved in protocol).

In *PPPDCP*, the customer uses his real identity C only in messages 1 and 2 from *SPayment* sub-protocol steps and in *Resolution* sub-protocols when he sends to CB the canceling request for recovering the coin's value. In both cases, only CB knows the real customer's identity C, and this is necessary to allow CB to provide a valid coin to the customer and perform the recovering of coin's value. To maintain the customer's privacy in *SPayment* sub-protocol, an electronic cash system based on blind digital signatures is used. CB's blind digital signature on the digital coin requested by the customer guarantees that CB cannot link the real identity of customer C with the digital coin bought by him: CB knows that C has bought a digital coin of some value, but without knowing the digital coin. In order not to relate the buyer C of a coin with the transaction in which his coin was canceled, we use a suitable coin's canceling way in *Resolution* sub-protocols. The coin's canceling request sent by C to CB includes *TTP*'s digital signature on a timestamp and the coin's value (only after TTP has checked the corresponding aborted payment evidence PE), without revealing the coin to CB.

The customer communicates with M using *Tor* anonymous network which does not allow another party (except the customer) to deduce that the customer sends PO to M. That's why, the customer chooses a different pseudo-identity C' and a corresponding public key PkC' in any subtransaction in which he communicates with M; both of them do not reveal any sensitive customer data.

The customer's privacy in *SDelivery* sub-protocol is ensured by considering DC from where the customer collects the physical product, only after he proves the knowledge of the access password set by M, without being necessary to disclose any information about his real identity.

As a result, customer's anonymity is preserved, and no party and no coalition between parties cannot link the true identity of the customer, C, with the pseudo-identity C'.

2.4 Comparative Analysis

A comparative analysis with regard to security properties of e-commerce protocols for physical product purchase is shown in Table 2.4. We remark that if we do not want the customer's privacy, the solution that meets all the other security requirements (effectiveness, strong fairness, timeliness, non-repudiation, integrity, and confidentiality) is the one described in Sect. 2.2. If in plus, we want to ensure the customer's privacy, then the most convenient solution is the one described in Sect. 2.3, because the other existing solutions either don't meet all the security requirements or consider a more complicated delivery business model which makes their applicability difficult.

Table 2.4 Comparative analysis of e-commerce protocols for buying physical products

Protocols	Zhang et al. [44]	*SP* Sect. 2.2	AlTawy et al. [6]	*PPPDCP* Sect. 2.3
Effectiveness	No	Yes	Yes	Yes
Strong Fairness	Yes	Yes	Partial	Yes
Timeliness	No	Yes	Yes	Yes
Non-repudiation	Yes	Yes	Yes	Yes
Integrity	Yes	Yes	Yes	Yes
Confidentiality	Yes	Yes	Yes	Yes
Customer's Privacy	No	No	Yes	Yes

References

1. Aimeur, E., Brassard, G., Mani Onana, F.: Secure anonymous physical delivery. IADIS Int. J. WWW/Internet **4**(1), 55–69 (2006)
2. Alaraj, A.: Fairness in physical products delivery protocol. Int. J. Comput. Netw. Commun. **4**(6), 99–110 (2012)
3. Alaraj, A., Munro, M.: An efficient fair exchange protocol that enforces the merchant to be honest. In: Proceedings of the IEEE International Conference on Collaborative Computing: Networking, Applications and Worksharing 2007, CollaborateCom 2007, USA, pp. 196–202 (2007)
4. Alaraj, A., Munro, M.: An e-commerce fair exchange protocol that enforces the customer to be honest. Int. J. Prod. Lifecycle Manag. **3**(2/3), 114–131 (2008)
5. Alaraj, A.M., Munro, M.: Enforcing honesty in fair exchange protocols. In: Badr, Y., Chbeir, R., Abraham, A., Hassanien, A.E. (eds.) Emergent Web Intelligence: Advanced Semantic Technologies. Advanced Information and Knowledge Processing. Springer, London (2010). https://doi.org/10.1007/978-1-84996-077-9_17
6. AlTawy, R., ElSheikh, M., Youssef, A.M., Gong, G.: Lelantos: A blockchain-based anonymous physical delivery system. In: 15th Annual Conference on Privacy, Security and Trust (PST), pp. 15–1509 (2017). https://doi.org/10.1109/PST.2017.00013
7. Amazon Hub Locker. https://www.amazon.com/primeinsider/tips/amazon-locker-qa.html. Cited June 25, 2022
8. Androulaki, E., Bellovin, S.: APOD: anonymous physical object delivery. In: Goldberg, I., Atallah, M.J. (eds.) Privacy Enhancing Technologies. PETS 2009. Lecture Notes in Computer Science, vol. 5672. Springer, Berlin, Heidelberg (2009). https://doi.org/10.1007/978-3-642-03168-7_12
9. Asokan, N., Schunter, M., Waidner, M.: Optimistic protocols for fair exchange. In: Proceedings of the 4th ACM Conference on Computer and Communications Security, pp. 7–17 (1997). https://doi.org/10.1145/266420.266426
10. Bîrjoveanu, C.V.: Anonymity and fair-exchange in e-commerce protocol for physical products delivery. In: Proceedings of the 12th International Conference on Security and Cryptography—SECRYPT, (ICETE 2015), pp. 170–177. SCITEPRESS (2015). https://doi.org/10.5220/0005508801700177
11. Bîrjoveanu, C.V., Bîrjoveanu, M.: Automated verification of e-commerce protocols for complex transactions. In: Obaidat, M. (ed.) E-Business and Telecommunications. ICETE 2018. Communications in Computer and Information Science, vol. 1118, pp. 87–110. Springer, Cham (2019). https://doi.org/10.1007/978-3-030-34866-3_5

12. Camenisch, J., Stadler, M.: Efficient group signature schemes for large groups. In: Kaliski, B.S. (ed.) Advances in Cryptology—CRYPTO '97. Lecture Notes in Computer Science, vol. 1294. Springer, Berlin, Heidelberg (1997). https://doi.org/10.1007/BFb0052252
13. Cao, T., Lin, D., Xue, R.: A randomized RSA-based partially blind signature scheme for electronic cash. Comput. Secur. **24**(1), 44–49 (2005)
14. Chaum, D: Untraceable electronic mail, return addresses, and digital pseudonyms. Commun. ACM **4**(2), 84–88 (1981)
15. Chaum, D.: Blind signatures for untraceable payments. In: Chaum, D., Rivest, R.L., Sherman, A.T. (eds.) Advances in Cryptology Proceedings of Crypto 82, Plenum. Springer, Berlin, pp. 199–203 (1982)
16. Chaum, D.: Security without identification: transaction systems to make big brother obsolete. Commun. ACM **28**(10), 1030–1044 (1985)
17. Diffie, W., Hellman, M.E.: New directions in cryptography. IEEE Trans. Inform. Theory **22**(6), 644–654 (1976)
18. Dingledine, R., Mathewson, N., Syverson, P.: Tor: the second-generation onion router. In: Proceedings of the 13th USENIX Security Symposium (2004)
19. Djuric, Z., Gasevic, D.: FEIPS: a secure fair-exchange payment system for internet transactions. Comput. J. **58**(10), 2537–2556 (2015)
20. Ethereum: Community guides and resources. https://ethereum.org/en/learn/. Cited June 25, 2022
21. Ethereum Whitepaper. https://ethereum.org/en/whitepaper/. Cited June 25, 2022
22. Küpçü, A., Lysyanskaya, A.: Usable optimistic fair exchange. In: Pieprzyk, J. (ed.) Topics in Cryptology—CT-RSA 2010. Lecture Notes in Computer Science, vol. 5985. Springer, Berlin, Heidelberg (2010). https://doi.org/10.1007/978-3-642-11925-5_18
23. Lin, S.J., Liu, D.C.: A fair-exchange and customer-anonymity electronic commerce protocol for digital content transactions. In: Janowski, T., Mohanty, H. (eds.) Distributed Computing and Internet Technology. ICDCIT 2007. Lecture Notes in Computer Science, vol. 4882. Springer, Berlin, Heidelberg (2007). https://doi.org/10.1007/978-3-540-77115-9_34
24. Lysyanskaya, A., Ramzan, Z.: Group blind digital signatures: a scalable solution to electronic cash. In: Hirchfeld, R. (ed.) Financial Cryptography. FC 1998. Lecture Notes in Computer Science, vol. 1465. Springer, Berlin, Heidelberg (1998). https://doi.org/10.1007/BFb0055483
25. Mars, A., Adi, W.: Fair exchange and anonymous e-commerce by deploying clone-resistant tokens. In: 2019 42nd International Convention on Information and Communication Technology, Electronics and Microelectronics (MIPRO), pp. 1226–1231 (2019). https://doi.org/10.23919/MIPRO.2019.8756734
26. Murdoch, S.J., Danezis, D.: Low-cost traffic analysis of Tor. In: 2005 IEEE Symposium on Security and Privacy (S&P'05), pp. 183–195 (2005). https://doi.org/10.1109/SP.2005.12
27. NIST: Federal Information Processing Standards Publication 197, Advanced Encryption Standard (AES) (2001). http://csrc.nist.gov/publications/fips/fips197/fips-197.pdf. Cited June 25, 2022
28. NIST: Federal Information Processing Standards Publication 180–4, Secure Hash Standard (SHS) (2015). https://nvlpubs.nist.gov/nistpubs/FIPS/NIST.FIPS.180-4.pdf. Cited June 25, 2022
29. Private Box. https://www.privatebox.co.nz/. Cited June 25, 2022
30. Ray, I., Ray, I.: An optimistic fair exchange e-commerce protocol with automated dispute resolution. In: Proceedings of 1st Electronic Commerce and Web Technologies Conference EC-Web 2000. Lecture Notes in Computer Science, vol. 1875, pp. 84–93. Springer, Berlin (2000)
31. Ray, I., Ray, I.: An anonymous fair-exchange e-commerce protocol. In: Proceedings 15th International Parallel and Distributed Processing Symposium, pp. 1790–1797 (2001)
32. Ray, I., Ray, I., Narasimhamurthi, N.: A fair-exchange e-commerce protocol with automated dispute resolution. In: Proceedings of the 14th Annual IFIP WG 11.3 Working Conference on Database Security, The Netherlands, pp. 27–38 (2001)

33. Ray, I., Ray, I., Narasimhamurthy, N.: An anonymous failure resilient fair-exchange ecommerce protocol. Decis. Support Syst. **39**(3), 267–292 (2005)
34. Reiter, M.K., Rubin, A.D.: Crowds: anonymity for web transactions. ACM Trans. Inform. Syst. Secur. **1**(1), 66–92 (1998). https://doi.org/10.1145/290163.290168
35. Rivest, R.L., Shamir, A., Adleman, L.: A method for obtaining digital signatures and public-key cryptosystems. Commun. ACM **21**(2), 120–126 (1978)
36. Ship Anon: Anonymous Shipping Service For Online Purchases. https://shipanon.com/. Cited June 25, 2022
37. Szabo, N.: Formalizing and securing relationships on public networks. First Monday **2**(9) (1997). https://doi.org/10.5210/fm.v2i9.548
38. Tor Server Metrics. https://metrics.torproject.org/networksize.html. Cited June 25, 2022
39. Vigano, L.: Automated security protocol analysis with the AVISPA tool. Electron. Notes Theor. Comput. Sci. **155**, 61–86 (2006). https://doi.org/10.1016/j.entcs.2005.11.052
40. Wang, S., Tang, X., Zhang, Y., Chen, J.: Auditable Protocols for fair payment and physical asset delivery based on smart contracts. IEEE Access **7**, 109439–109453 (2019). https://doi.org/10.1109/ACCESS.2019.2933860
41. Wood, G.: Ethereum: A Secure Decentralised Generalised Transaction Ledger. https://ethereum.github.io/yellowpaper/paper.pdf. Cited June 25, 2022
42. Xia, Y., Chen, R., Su, J., Zou, H.: Balancing anonymity and resilience in anonymous communication networks. Comput. Secur. **101**, 102106 (2021)
43. Zhang, N., Shi, Q., Merabti, M.: An efficient protocol for anonymous and fair document exchange. Comput. Netw. **41**(1), 19–28 (2003)
44. Zhang, Q., Markantonakis, K., Mayes, K.: A practical fair exchange e-payment protocol for anonymous purchase and physical delivery. In: Proceedings of the 4th ACS/IEEE International Conference on Computer Systems and Applications, AICCSA-06, UAE, pp. 851–858 (2006)

Chapter 3
Multi-party E-Commerce Protocols for Complex Transactions

3.1 State-of-the-Art Analysis

Many fair exchange solutions that take into consideration *multi-party* scenarios are known, with applications in e-commerce transactions for buying physical goods [4–6, 8], buying digital goods [7, 15], exchange of digital items [1, 2, 12–14], digital signature of contracts [10, 11, 16], non-repudiation [17, 18], and certified email [17, 19].

Asokan et al. [1] propose the first protocol involving multiple parties, which allows each party to perform a fair exchange of digital items and non-repudiation evidences with all other parties. The protocol is generic; the digital items can be digital signatures, electronic payments and digital goods, or data. The authors use a global matrix of item's descriptions that will be exchanged between all parties. The parties undertake to send the items to other parties by signing the global matrix of item's descriptions. Only after all participants sign the same global matrix, the exchange of the promised items takes place. The protocol uses a *TTP* if some exceptions appear (a party receives an item or a non-repudiation evidence that is not correct), in which case *TTP* sends an affidavit to all involved parties. So, this solution guarantees effectiveness, weak fairness, and timeliness. The authors state that strong fairness can be ensured only if *TTP* has the ability to revoke or replace the items. However, we consider that this condition is unusual in real-world applications, because on the one side a user is unlikely to want to change the item it wants with another and on the other side this ability of *TTP* goes far beyond the usual way it is involved in resolving disputes. The solution is not efficient from a practical point of view, as a large amount of information should be broadcasted.

In [14], Kılınç et al. propose a solution for the fair exchange of digital items between multiple parties, which removes the restriction of Asokan et al.'s solution from [1] where each party exchanges items with all other parties. Thus, the solution from [14] can be applied on an arbitrary exchange topology, which does not restrict the items received by the involved parties. For example, the party P_1 wants an item

C. V. Bîrjoveanu, M. Bîrjoveanu, *Secure Multi-Party E-Commerce Protocols*, SpringerBriefs in Computer Science, https://doi.org/10.1007/978-3-030-99351-1_3

from the party P_2 and an item from the party P_3, but P_2 and P_3 do not want to exchange any items. Also, the solution proposed by Kılınç et al. does not require a broadcast, being more efficient than the solution proposed in [1]. The major disadvantage of the solution from [14] (as well as from [1]) is that the exchanged items are considered generic, without describing how this solution can be applied for a multi-party scenario in which a party wants to buy digital items from some other parties.

In [2, 12, 13], the authors analyze the exchange of digital items, using an exchange ring topology, in which each party sends an item to the next party from the ring and receives an item from the previous party from the ring. The solution proposed by Franklin et al. [12] uses an online *TTP*, while the solution of Bao et al. [2] is based on an offline *TTP*. The protocol proposed by Bao et al. consists of two rounds. In the first round, each party P_i (beginning with the initiator) sends to the next party P_{i+1} a cipher c_i obtained using the *TTP*'s public key together with a certificate proving that c_i represents the encryption of the valid item which P_{i+1} wants to acquire. After the first round is completed, during the second round, each party P_i (beginning with the initiator) sends to the next party P_{i+1} the promised item. If a party P_i doesn't receive the corresponding item, then it initiates a *Recovery protocol* with *TTP*, which in his turn contacts the protocol's initiator to confirm the successful finish of the first round of the protocol. If the initiator provides a positive answer, then *TTP* decrypts c_i for P_i. We remark that fairness definition from [2, 13] is an *incomplete* fairness defined as follows: after protocol execution, no party will send the item to the next party without receiving the item from the previous party. So, this concept of fairness allows that some parties receive the desired item and some other parties don't. This definition differs to fairness considered in [1, 14] and in all solutions detailed presented in this book for multi-party scenarios in which either all parties receive the desired item or none of them nothing. We consider that the *incomplete* fairness is in contradiction with the multi-party scenario itself, where fairness should be defined taking into consideration the involved multiple parties. Also, the *incomplete* fairness is more suitable for independent multi two-party scenarios. Another problem with the protocol from [2] is that, using *Recovery protocol*, the protocol's initiator can collude with some parties to exclude some other parties from the exchange. This leads to the requirement that the protocol's participants should trust both *TTP* and initiator. This problem was fixed by the protocol proposed by González-Deleito et al. [13], which removes the trust in the initiator requirement.

Digital signature of contracts considering multi-party scenarios in that all parties fairly exchange their signatures on the same pre-agreed contract is proposed by Mukhamedov et al. in [16], using an offline *TTP*, and by Ferrer-Gomila et al. in [11], using *Ethereum blockchain*. The multi-party contract signing protocol proposed in [11] consists of three sub-protocols: *Exchange*, *Finish*, and *Query*. Two rounds are executed in the *Exchange* sub-protocol. In the first round, the parties send the signatures back and forth, as follows: the first signatory sends its signature on the contract to the second signatory, which in turn sends to the third signatory its signature and the signature received from the first signatory, and so on, until the last signatory receives the signatures of all other parties. Then, the signatures will be sent in the reverse order, from the last signatory sending his signature to the previous one, and so on, until the first signatory receives the signatures of all other parties. If the first round is successfully finished, then each party will have the signatures of all other parties. But this does not mean that the contract is signed. To get a contract signing proof, a second round will be executed, in which the parties exchange the acknowledgments (in the same way as in the first round) of the fact that each party has received, in the first round, signatures from all other parties. After the success of the second round, each party has a proof of signing the contract: each party will have the confirmation of receipt from all other parties. *Finish* and *Query* sub-protocols are executed on the blockchain, only in the cases in which after *Exchange* sub-protocol execution, a party does not know if the contract has been signed or not. So, if the first round of the *Exchange* sub-protocol is successful for a party P_i, but in the second round it doesn't receive the acknowledgment from all other parties, then it does not have a contract signing proof. In this case, P_i initiates *Finish* sub-protocol by invoking the *finish* function of the smart contact, which will store the signatures of all parties and will set the status of the contract as signed. Also, if after the first round execution of the *Exchange* sub-protocol, a party P_j has sent his signature, but did not receive the signatures from all the other parties, then P_j does not know the status of the contract. In this case, P_j initiates *Query* sub-protocol which is executed on the blockchain, by invoking the *query* function of the smart contact. The result of the *query* call depends on the information stored by the smart contract. Thus, if the smart contract has stored the signatures of all parties (after a certain party has executed *Finish* sub-protocol), then it will return the signatures, and P_j will know that the contract has been signed. Otherwise, if the smart contract does not have these signatures, then he will inform P_j, and then P_j will know that the contract has not been signed. After protocol run, fairness is ensured: either all parties get the signature on the contract, or none gets the signature on the contract. Also, effectiveness regarding the usage of blockchain, timeliness, and non-repudiation is guaranteed. Multi-party contract signing can be used in certain e-commerce transactions involving multiple parties. But, the major disadvantage of the protocols proposed in [11, 16] is that these are used in scenarios in which all parties involved know each other, which drastically limits their applicability.

Draper-Gil et al. [10] present a multi-party contract signing protocol, where a customer wants to sign different contracts with many providers, pairwise, providing atomicity. So, the customer is interested to obtain the signature on contracts from all providers. This scenario is different from the one considered in [11, 16], by the fact that the customer wants to sign many different contracts, and the customer knows each provider, but the providers do not know each other. The solution described in [10] is composed of two sub-protocols: *Exchange* and *Resolution*. *Exchange* sub-protocol is executed in n rounds, where n is the number of parties involved in the protocol. In each round, the customer sends a *commitment* (a customer's signature) corresponding to that round, to each provider, and waits for a corresponding *acceptance* (a provider's signature) from each provider, before participating in the next round. After the execution of the nth round, each party has the evidence that its contract has been signed, represented by the commitments and acceptances received in the round n. *Resolution* sub-protocol is used to ensure fairness and atomicity. If the customer does not receive one of the acceptances in a round $r > 1$, then he will contact *TTP* to receive, after the *Resolution* execution, either $n - 1$ signed tokens or $n - 1$ canceled token (tokens are generated by *TTP* by signing) corresponding to the $n - 1$ contracts. Also, if a provider claims that it does not received a commitment corresponding to some round, then it will contact *TTP* to receive, after *Resolution* execution, either a signed or canceled token. The protocol provides effectiveness, weak fairness, timeliness, non-repudiation, and confidentiality, but we consider that it is quite complicated, having a significant number of messages that must be transmitted.

Onieva et al. describe in [18] a multi-party protocol based on an online *TTP*, which allows a sender to send different messages to multiple recipients, providing the fair exchange of non-repudiation evidences. The sender sends to each recipient the encrypted message and the evidence of origin corresponding to the encrypted message. After the sender receives the evidence of reception corresponding to the encrypted message from some recipients denoted by the set R, it sends the suitable key for message decryption to *TTP*, where each recipient from R can take it and get the message. In [17], Onieva et al. extend the solution from [18] to an optimistic non-repudiation protocol that allows a sender to send different messages to multiple recipients. In this extension, *TTP* is involved in protocol only in the situations when a party does not receive the correct message or evidence. Thus, if a recipient in R does not receive the suitable decryption key from the sender, then it can get it from *TTP*. Both solutions proposed in [17, 18] ensure non-repudiation, strong fairness, and timeliness, but do not provide atomicity. The protocols allow the parties to exchange only different generic messages; as a result, their applicability cases for multi-party e-commerce transactions are missing.

In [15], Liu proposes a multi-party protocol, where a customer wants to buy several digital products from different merchants in an aggregate transaction. The protocol is composed of *Exchange* sub-protocol and three *Resolution* sub-protocols. In the *Exchange* sub-protocol, for each product in the product package, the customer receives the product, and after he is satisfied with it, he sends the payment to the corresponding merchant. The author claims that the protocol provides fairness, but the proposed protocol allows the following scenario: the customer can get some products from the package in *Exchange* sub-protocol and for the other products from the package get only affidavits from *TTP* by running the corresponding *Resolution* sub-protocols. However, an affidavit represents only a form of compensation (in money) for the customer from dishonest merchants, but not the required digital product as a component of a product's package. As a result, this protocol can be used only for a partial transaction, in which the customer is interested to buy only some products from the package, not necessarily all the products from the package. We consider that an aggregate transaction requires more than this protocol offers, namely, the customer should obtain all products from the package, or none of them. Also, timeliness and confidentiality requirements are not assured. Bîrjoveanu et al. [7] propose a multi-party e-commerce protocol for buying digital products, where the customer wants to acquire different digital products from many merchants in *complex transactions*. The combination in any form of aggregate and optional transactions defines a complex transaction. Every merchant who wants to sell his product will provide a digital certificate of the product on the online catalog. The product's digital certificate is generated by a certificate authority which signs the product's description information and the hybrid encryption of the product using the payment gateway's public key. The protocol is composed of *Payment*, *Delivery*, and *Resolution* sub-protocols. In *Payment* sub-protocol, the customer pays to the merchants the products corresponding to the complex transaction in which he was engaged. After *Payment* sub-protocol, the customer gets either the receipts from all successful subtransactions or aborted evidences corresponding to all aborted subtransactions. To provide fairness in complex transactions, *Delivery* sub-protocol is applied only after the successful completion of *Payment* sub-protocol. Thus, in *Delivery* sub-protocol, the merchant sends the decryption key of the product corresponding to each successful subtransaction from *Payment* sub-protocol. In the case in which the customer receives an incorrect decryption key from a merchant, then he can obtain the appropriate product decryption key from payment gateway, which in turn knows it from the product's digital certificate. The protocol ensures effectiveness, strong fairness, timeliness, non-repudiation, integrity, and confidentiality.

Section 3.4 presents an extension of the *Complex Transactions Protocol* from [6]. The e-commerce protocols from [4, 6] consider complex transactions in that the customer wants to buy a set of physical products from different merchants, in which the complex transactions are combinations in any form of aggregate and optional transactions. We extend the complex transactions from [4, 6] to include also the *partial transactions*.

In Sect. 3.5, we describe an e-commerce *Complex Transaction Protocol Providing Customer's Privacy* (*CTPCP*) for physical products delivery which improves the solution from [5]. An extension of the solution from [5], which obtains the anonymity of the involved merchants besides the customer's anonymity, is presented in [8].

3.2   B2B and B2C Use Cases

In this section, we describe use cases for the multi-party e-commerce protocols detailed in the following sections of this chapter. In a B2B scenario, Creative Art is a firm which activity is art creative crafts in small series. To start the next project, Creative Art prepares the materials it needs, browsing on the online catalog where different merchants M_1, M_2, etc. promote their products. First, it would need a soft plywood: the first option for this is cedar plywood (cp) from M_1, but if due to delivery time or lack of stock this is not possible, then its second option is pine plywood (pp) from M_2. Next, it needs rice paper with a floral theme: the first option would be a rice paper with a lavender theme (rpl) from M_3, the second option is a rice paper with a rose theme (rpr) from M_4, and the third option is a rice paper with a tulip theme (rpt) from M_3. It also needs a combination between decorative ribbon and decorative cord. For this project, it needs at least one of the following combinations, but if they are available, it can acquire all specified combinations for further product variations: the first combination is red ribbon (rr) and white cord (wc) from M_5, the second combination is yellow ribbon (yr) and red cord (rc) from M_6, and the third combination is blue ribbon (br) and silver cord (sc) from M_7. To assemble and finish the products, it will need also adhesive (ad) from M_1 and varnish (va) and white paint (wp) from M_8. To start crafting the new product, Creative Art will need exactly one type of plywood, exactly one type of rice paper, at least one combination of decorative ribbon and decorative cord, adhesive, varnish, and paint. Creative Art creates its order in the form of an e-commerce complex transaction like below:

$$(cp \vee pp) \wedge (rpl \vee rpr \vee rpt) \wedge ((rr \wedge wc) * (yr \wedge rc) * (br \wedge sc)) \wedge ad \wedge va \wedge wp$$

In the above complex transaction, $\wedge$, $\vee$, and $*$ denote the transaction operators used to represent aggregate, optional, and partial transaction, respectively. These operators are defined in Sect. 3.4. The complex transaction is an aggregate transaction in which the first two components of it are optional transactions (cp $\vee$ pp and rpl $\vee$ rpr $\vee$ rpt), the third component is the partial transaction ((rr $\wedge$ wc) $*$ (yr $\wedge$ rc) $*$ (br $\wedge$ sc)), and the rest of the components are individual products. The partial transaction has three component aggregate transactions. An example in which the complex transaction is successfully completed is when after Creative Art sends his order, he receives the pack: cp, rpl, (rr, wc), (yr, rc), ad, va, and wp. If Creative Art successfully acquires cp but does not acquire any of the products rpl, rpr, or rpt of the optional transaction (rpl $\vee$ rpr $\vee$ rpt), then the entire complex transaction is not successful because Creative Art does not have all the components needed to manufacture its products. Also, Creative Art should not purchase more than one product from any optional transaction from the complex transaction, because otherwise it would be left with products that it does not use. In the partial transaction ((rr $\wedge$ wc) $*$ (yr $\wedge$ rc) $*$ (br $\wedge$ sc)), Creative Art needs to purchase at least one of the three combinations, but because he wants to vary the design of the product, he is also satisfied with two or all three combinations. If Creative Art does not buy all the combinations from the partial transaction (but at least one combination is bought), then for the other combinations, it might have alternatives.

In a B2C scenario, instead of the firm Creative Art, it is a person who wants to do a creative craft for himself/herself.

3.3 Security Requirements

To design secure multi-party e-commerce protocols for complex transactions, we need to define the corresponding security requirements. Authentication, authorization, integrity, non-repudiation, confidentiality, and customer's privacy are defined for multi-party e-commerce protocols by direct extension of the corresponding properties defined in Sect. 1.3 for two-party e-commerce protocols. We must pay special attention to strong fairness, effectiveness, and timeliness in multi-party e-commerce scenarios. Consequently, in what follows, we will adapt these security requirements from two-party scenarios to multi-party scenarios.

Strong Fairness. A multi-party e-commerce protocol/a multi-party e-commerce protocol with physical product delivery ensures strong fairness if after the protocol execution, the following statements are met:

- For any optional transaction from the complex transaction, the customer obtains exactly one successful payment evidence/physical product for the product's payment, and
- For any aggregate transaction from the complex transaction, the customer obtains successful payment evidences/physical products for the payments of all products, and
- For any partial transaction from the complex transaction, the customer obtains at least one successful payment evidence/physical product for the corresponding payment

and each merchant obtains the corresponding payment for the product, or none of them obtains nothing.

Effectiveness requires that if every party involved in the multi-party e-commerce protocol behaves honestly and no communication error occurs, then after protocol execution, the customer receives his successful payment evidences/physical products from merchants, and the merchants receive their payments from the customer without any intervention of *TTP*.

Timeliness requires that any party involved in the multi-party e-commerce protocol can be sure that the protocol execution will be finished at a certain finite point of time without losing strong fairness.

3.4 Complex Transaction Protocol

Our *Complex Transactions Protocol* (*CTP*) in which one customer can buy products in complex transactions from many merchants extends the complex transactions as being the combinations in any form of aggregate, optional, and partial transactions. *CTP* has the following participants: the customer C, the merchants $M_1, \ldots, M_n$, the payment gateway PG, and the customer bank CB. A complex transaction run considering a customer and many merchants means running a subtransactions sequence considering a customer and one merchant in any subtransaction. Running of the subtransactions sequence is performed under a set of constraints depending of the combination of the aggregate, optional, and partial transactions from the complex transaction. Thus, *CTP* uses *Subtransaction Protocol* (*SP*) from Sect. 2.2. We make the same considerations as for *SP* regarding communication channels set between parties and public key digital certificates of the involved parties in *CTP*.

In what follows, we define the *transaction operators*, which are necessary for *CTP* to express the products that the customer wants to buy in an aggregate, optional, or partial transaction from a complex transaction.

Definition 3.1 The *aggregation* operator, denoted by $\wedge$, is used for an aggregate transaction, as follows: $Pid_1 \wedge \ldots \wedge Pid_k$ meaning that the customer wishes to buy exactly k products with product's identifiers $Pid_1, \ldots, Pid_k$.

Definition 3.2 The *option* operator, denoted by $\vee$, is used for an optional transaction as follows: $Pid_1 \vee \ldots \vee Pid_k$ meaning that the customer wishes to buy exactly one of the products with product's identifiers $Pid_1, \ldots, Pid_k$. The customer wishes first of all to buy the product Pid_1, but if this is not possible, his second option is Pid_2, and so on. Thus, the customer provides the products' purchase priority by the order of their appearance.

Definition 3.3 The *part* operator, denoted by $*$, is used for a partial transaction, as follows: $Pid_1 * \ldots * Pid_k$ meaning that the customer wishes to buy at least one of the products with identifiers $Pid_1, \ldots, Pid_k$. In a partial transaction, the customer wishes to buy at least one from k products for which he has expressed his intention to buy them. A partial transaction is necessary to be considered in the following scenario: the customer wishes to buy $k \geq 1$ products from favorites merchants, but he is satisfied even if only a part of k products are successfully bought. For the other products that are not acquired, the customer might have other alternatives.

We consider an online catalog where products from merchants are posted and where the user browses to search for the products he is interested in. The user provides in the form of a complex transaction the products pack he wants to buy, the options/alternatives for each product from the pack, and what product subpackage can be partially purchased. On "submit," the payment Web segment builds a *transaction tree* associated with the complex transaction provided by the user.

The transaction tree is built over the product identifiers selected by the user and $\wedge$, $\vee$, and $*$ operators. For the transaction tree representation, we use the *left-child, right-sibling representation* based on [9]. Each internal node corresponds to one of the above operators or to a product identifier, while each leaf node corresponds to a product identifier. Each node of the tree is represented by a structure with the following fields:

- *info* for storing the node type: product identifier or one of the operators
- *left* for pointing to the leftmost child of node
- *right* for pointing to the sibling of the node immediately to the right

The access to the tree is realized through the root.

The left-child, right-sibling representation has several advantages. First, this representation allows each node of the tree to have a variable number of children, which is suitable for our goal of representing a tree associated with a complex transaction in which each aggregate, optional, or partial transaction may have a variable number of component products. Second, each node has maximum two

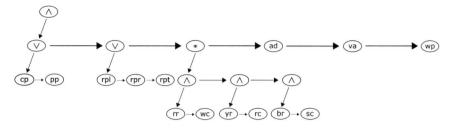

Fig. 3.1 Transaction tree associated with a complex transaction

references: to his leftmost child and to his sibling immediately to the right. This makes *CTP* much easier and efficient to implement.

Figure 3.1 illustrates the transaction tree associated with the complex transaction from Sect. 3.2, where cp is the identifier for cedar plywood, pp for pine plywood, wp for white paint, and so on. The root node has $\wedge$ operator as *info*. The root does not have any right sibling, and its children are two nodes having $\vee$ operator as *info*, a node having $*$ operator as *info*, and three nodes with the *info* ad, va, and wp, respectively. A parent-child link is realized as follows: the parent node points only to its leftmost child, while the rest of its children can be accessed starting with the leftmost child via sibling relationship. The leftmost child of the root is the first node (from left) having as information the option operator, the second node having as information the option operator is the right sibling of the leftmost child, the node with the information the part operator is the right sibling of the second node having as information the option operator, the node with the information wp is the right sibling of the node having as information va, and the node with the information wp does not have any right sibling.

Definition 3.4 A subtransaction s, denoted by $SP(C, M_i, Pid_l)$, is an instance of *Subtransaction Protocol* in which the customer C buys from the merchant M_i the physical product with Pid_l identifier.

For a subtransaction $s = SP(C, M_i, Pid_l)$, we denote by $Pe(s)$ the payment evidence PE that C will receive after running of s. $Pe(s).Resp$ denotes the response ($Resp$) in $Pe(s)$.

Definition 3.5 The state of a node p, denoted by $St(p)$, is the sequence of payment evidences $Pe(s_1) \ldots Pe(s_m)$ from the subtransactions $s_1 \ldots s_m$ initiated by C for buying the product defined by p. $St(p)$ is calculated depending on $p \rightarrow info$, as follows:

- $p \rightarrow info = Pid_l$

    For a node p that has as information a product identifier Pid_l, the state $St(p)$ is the payment evidence received by C in the subtransaction in which he buys the product with the identifier Pid_l. So, $St(p) = Pe(SP(C, M_i, Pid_l))$.

Fig. 3.2 State of a node p
with $\vee$ operator as *info*

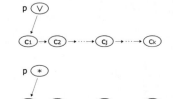

Fig. 3.3 State of a node p
with $*$ operator as *info*

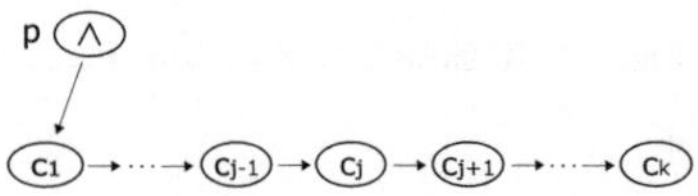

Fig. 3.4 State of a node p
with $\wedge$ operator as *info*

- $p \rightarrow info = \vee$, and $c_1, \ldots, c_k$ are the children of p

  This case is illustrated in Fig. 3.2. The appearance order of the children of p from left to the right—c_1, c_2, and so on until c_k—provides the customer priority in products purchase. So, if there is c_j the leftmost child of p for which $St(c_j)$ contains only successful subtransaction payment evidences (meaning that $Pe(s).Resp = YES$, for all $Pe(s) \in St(c_j)$), then $St(p) = St(c_j)$.

  Otherwise, if all subtransaction payment evidences from node states of all p's children are aborted (meaning that $Pe(s).Resp = ABORT$, for all $Pe(s) \in St(c_j)$, for all $1 \leq j \leq k$), then $St(p) = St(c_k)$, meaning the node state of the rightmost child c_k of p.

- $p \rightarrow info = *$, and $c_1, \ldots, c_k$ are the children of p

  In such a case, illustrated in Fig. 3.3, the customer wishes to buy at least one of the products represented by the children of the node p. So, after running all the subtransactions corresponding to the children c_1, c_2, and so on until c_k, the state $St(p)$ consists of the sequence of all $St(c_j)$, where $1 \leq j \leq k$, for that all subtransaction payment evidences from $St(c_j)$ are successful. Otherwise, if all payment evidences of the subtransactions from node states of all children of p are aborted, then $St(p) = St(c_k)$, meaning the node state of the rightmost child c_k of p.

- $p \rightarrow info = \wedge$, and $c_1, \ldots, c_k$ are all children of p

  Figure 3.4 describes this case. If all subtransaction payment evidences from node states of all children of p are successful, then $St(p)$ is the sequence of all node states of p's children. Thus, $St(p) = St(c_1) \ldots St(c_k)$.

  Otherwise, if there is c_j, the leftmost child of p such that all subtransaction payment evidences from $St(c_j)$ are aborted, then the node states $St(c_{j+1}) \ldots St(c_k)$ will no longer be calculated. This is because the aggregate transaction corresponding to the node p is aborted. In this case, $St(p)$ is the sequence of node states of p's children c_1, c_2, and so on until c_j. So, $St(p) = St(c_1) \ldots St(c_j)$. We remark that the node states $St(c_1) \ldots St(c_{j-1})$ contain only successful subtransaction payment evidences. So, to maintain fairness, all these subtransactions will be aborted.

As we can see, $St(p)$ contains a sequence of subtransaction payment evidences in which either all payment evidences are successful or all are aborted.

Algorithm 3.1 describes the *Complex Transaction Protocol*. For the root t of the transaction tree associated with the complex transaction provided by the user, *CTP* recursively calculates the node state $St(t)$. The transaction tree is traversed in a similar manner with depth-first search. For any node p of the transaction tree, Algorithm 3.1 uses a *child* array to store the node states of all p's children. Thus, $child[j]$ stores the node state of the j-th leftmost child of p. More exactly, $child[0]$ stores the node state of the leftmost child of p, $child[1]$ the node state of the sibling immediately to the right of $child[0]$, and so on.

Algorithm 3.1 computes $St(p)$ for a node p corresponding to $\vee$ and $\wedge$ operators, depending on some conditions that are satisfied w.r.t. $child[0]$ (lines 2–4). If the node p corresponds to $\vee$ operator and all payment evidences from $child[0]$ are successful (line 2), then $St(p)$ is $child[0]$. Also, if p corresponds to $\wedge$ operator and all payment evidences from $child[0]$ are aborted (line 3), then $St(p)$ is $child[0]$.

The node states $child[j]$ (with $j \geq 1$), for any child of a node p, where p has at least two children, are computed in the **while** loop (lines 6–14). The conditions from line 10 test scenario in which for a node p corresponding to $\wedge$ operator, there is the leftmost node state $child[j]$ of a child of p, where $j \geq 1$, containing only aborted payment evidences. This means that the node states of p's children $child[0], \ldots,$ $child[j-1]$ contain only successful payment evidences, but however the aggregate transaction corresponding to p is aborted. Thus, to ensure fairness, *AggregateAbort* sub-protocol is applied at line 12, to abort any successful subtransaction which has a successful payment evidence in $child[c]$, where $1 \leq c \leq j-1$. The *AggregateAbort* sub-protocol computes $ASt(p)$—the aborted $St(p)$. $ASt(p)$ is the payment evidences sequence consisting of the aborted payment evidences that aborts all successful payment evidences from $child[c]$, where $1 \leq c \leq j-1$, and the aborted payment evidences from $child[j]$. The *AggregateAbort* sub-protocol is described in Sect. 3.4.1.

The node state $St(p)$ for a node p with a product identifier Pid_l as *info* is calculated at line 15. If p is a node corresponding to $\vee$ operator, for which all payment evidences of all p's children are aborted, then $St(p)$ is computed at lines 16–19. The node state for a node that corresponds to $*$ operator is computed at lines 20–25. If the condition tested at line 24 is met (λ denotes the empty string), then all node states of p's children contain only aborted payment evidences. In this case, $St(p)$ is calculated as being the node state of the rightmost child of p. At the lines 26–27, Algorithm 3.1 calculates the node state for a node that corresponds to $\wedge$ operator for that all node states of p's children contain only successful payment evidences.

Algorithm 3.1 $CTP(t)$: complex transactions protocol

Input: Root t of the transaction tree associated with the complex transaction
Output: $St(t)$—State of t
1. **if** $(t \to left \neq NULL)$ $child[0] = CTP(t \to left)$;
2. **if** $((t \to info = \vee$ and $Pe(s).Resp = YES$, for all $Pe(s) \in child[0])$ or
3. $\qquad (t \to info = \wedge$ and $Pe(s).Resp = ABORT$, for all $Pe(s) \in child[0]))$
4. $\qquad\qquad St(t) = child[0]$; **return** $St(t)$;
5. $j = 1$; $k = t \to left \to right$;
6. **while** $(k \neq NULL)$
7. $\qquad child[j] = CTP(k)$;
8. $\qquad$ **if** $(t \to info = \vee$ and $Pe(s).Resp = YES$, for all $Pe(s) \in child[j])$
9. $\qquad\qquad St(t) = child[j]$; **return** $St(t)$;
10. $\qquad$ **if** $(t \to info = \wedge$ and $Pe(s).Resp = ABORT$, for all $Pe(s) \in child[j])$
11. $\qquad\qquad$ **for** $(c = 0; c \leq j; c = c + 1)$ $St(t) = St(t)child[c]$; **end for**
12. $\qquad\qquad AggregateAbort(St(t))$; **return** $ASt(t)$;
13. $\qquad k = k \to right$; $j = j + 1$;
14. **end while**
15. **if** $(t \to info = Pid_l)$ $St(t) = Pe(SP(C, M_i, Pid_l))$; **return** $St(t)$;
16. **else if** $(t \to info = \vee)$
17. $\qquad\qquad k = t \to left$;
18. $\qquad\qquad$ **while** $(k \to right \neq NULL)$ $k = k \to right$; **end while**
19. $\qquad\qquad St(t) = St(k)$; **return** $St(t)$;
20. $\qquad$ **else if** $(t \to info = *)$
21. $\qquad\qquad$ **for** $(c = 0; c \leq j - 1; c = c + 1)$
22. $\qquad\qquad\qquad$ **if** $(Pe(s).Resp = YES$, for all $Pe(s) \in child[c])$
23. $\qquad\qquad\qquad\qquad St(t) = St(t)child[c]$; **end for**
24. $\qquad\qquad\qquad$ **if** $(c = j$ and $St(t) = \lambda)$ $St(t) = child[c - 1]$;
25. $\qquad\qquad\qquad$ **return** $St(t)$;
26. $\qquad\qquad$ **else for** $(c = 0; c \leq j - 1; c = c + 1)$ $St(t) = St(t)child[c]$; **end for**
27. $\qquad\qquad\qquad$ **return** $St(t)$;
28. $\qquad\qquad$ **end if**
29. $\qquad$ **end if**
30. **end if**

3.4.1 AggregateAbort Sub-protocol

If in *CTP*, the conditions from line 10 of Algorithm 3.1 are met, then an unfair case for customer appears. In this case, there is a node p corresponding to $\wedge$ operator for which $child[j]$, where $j \geq 1$, is the leftmost node state of a child of p containing only aborted payment evidences. The customer is disadvantaged because he received successful payment evidences in all node states $child[c]$, with $1 \leq c \leq j - 1$.

Thus, $AggregateAbort(St(p))$ sub-protocol, where $St(p) = child[0] \ldots child[j - 1]child[j]$, is initiated by C to restore fairness by aborting all successful payment evidence from $child[c]$, with $1 \leq c \leq j - 1$. $AggregateAbort(St(p))$ sub-protocol messages are graphically represented in Fig. 3.5.

C sends to PG an *aggregate abort request* in message 1, which consists of $St(p)$ and his signature on $St(p)$, both encrypted with $PkPG$.

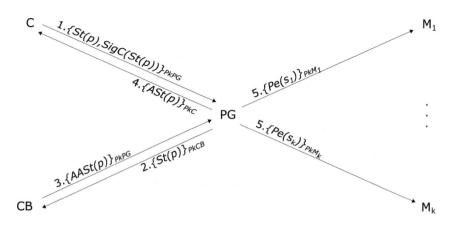

Fig. 3.5 *AggregateAbort*($St(p)$) sub-protocol message flow

Message 1: $C \rightarrow PG : \{St(p), SigC(St(p))\}_{PkPG}$

After PG receives the customer request, he obtains $St(p)$ by decrypting it and checks the request's authenticity by verifying C's signature. $St(p)$ is a sequence of payment evidences $Pe(s_1) \ldots Pe(s_k)Pe(s_{k+1}) \ldots Pe(s_m)$, where $Pe(s_i).Resp = YES$ for all $1 \le i \le k$ and $Pe(s_j).Resp = ABORT$ for all $k + 1 \le j \le m$. Also, for each payment evidence from $St(p)$, PG searches it in its database and checks his signature to verify the payment evidence's authenticity. If all these checks are successful, then PG sends $St(p)$ to the customer bank CB in message 2.

Message 2: $PG \rightarrow CB : \{St(p)\}_{PkCB}$

CB decrypts message 2, obtains $St(p)$, and checks the authenticity of each payment evidence from $St(p)$. If all checks are successfully passed, CB generates an aborted acknowledgment of $St(p)$, denoted by $AASt(p)$. For this, CB aborts each successful payment evidence $Pe(s_i)=YES, C, M_i, Id, SigPG(YES, C, M_i, Id, Am) \in St(p)$, where $1 \le i \le k$, as follows:

1. CB cancels the transfer corresponding to $Pe(s_i)$ from C's account into M_i's account.
2. CB generates the aborted acknowledgment payment evidence for $Pe(s_i)$, denoted $AAPe(s_i)$ as being
   $AAPe(s_i) = ABORT, C, M_i, Id, SigCB(ABORT, C, M_i, Id, Am, Pe(s_i))$.

CB computes the aborted acknowledgment of $St(p)$ by
$AASt(p) = AAPe(s_1) \ldots AAPe(s_k)Pe(s_{k+1}) \ldots Pe(s_m)$. Next, CB sends $AASt(p)$ to PG in message 3.

Message 3: $CB \rightarrow PG : \{AASt(p)\}_{PkPG}$

PG obtains $AASt(p)$ and, for each aborted acknowledgment payment evidence $AAPe(s_i) \in AASt(p)$, uses his signature to compute the corresponding aborted updated payment evidence, as follows: $Pe1(s_i) = Pe(s_i)$ and
$Pe(s_i) = ABORT, C, M_i, Id, SigPG(ABORT, C, M_i, Id, Am, Pe1(s_i))$. Further, PG computes the aborted $St(p)$ as being $ASt(p) = Pe(s_1) \ldots Pe(s_k)Pe(s_{k+1}) \ldots Pe(s_m)$ and sends it to C in message 4.

Message 4: $PG \rightarrow C : \{ASt(p)\}_{PkC}$

Also, in message 5, PG sends simultaneous each aborted payment evidence $Pe(s_i) \in ASt(p)$ to the corresponding merchant M_i, where $1 \le i \le k$.

Message 5: $PG \rightarrow M_i : \{Pe(s_i)\}_{PkM_i}$

As a result, all payment evidences from $St(p)$ were aborted, and fairness is ensured.

CTP Security Discussion

CTP provides all the security requirements that *SP* used in *CTP* provides: effectiveness, strong fairness, timeliness, non-repudiation, integrity, and confidentiality.

SP ensures effectiveness, non-repudiation, integrity, and confidentiality. So, any subtransaction carried out in *CTP* provides these security requirements. Therefore, *CTP* provides effectiveness, non-repudiation, integrity, and confidentiality.

Strong fairness in *CTP* requires strong fairness in *SP* as a minimum condition. However, strong fairness in *SP* does not necessarily lead to strong fairness in *CTP*. Thus, to obtain strong fairness in *CTP*, three additional conditions must be satisfied in *CTP* regarding strong fairness of different transaction types from which the complex transaction is formed. So, the first condition requires strong fairness in any optional transaction from complex transaction. This condition is satisfied in *CTP* by the way in which Algorithm 3.1 calculates the node state corresponding to $\vee$ operator in the transaction tree associated with the complex transaction. Secondly, strong fairness in any partial transaction from complex transaction is required. *CTP* satisfies this condition because the node state corresponding to $*$ operator in the transaction tree is computed such that either C gets at least one successful payment evidence from merchants and the corresponding merchants get payments from C or none of them gets nothing. Thirdly, strong fairness in any aggregate transaction from complex transaction is required. Algorithm 3.1 computes the node state corresponding to $\wedge$ operator so that there can be only one case in which strong fairness is not satisfied: the aggregate transaction is not successful, but C has received some successful payment evidences corresponding to the subtransactions from the aggregate transaction. Strong fairness is restored in this case, because *CTP* applies *AggregateAbort* sub-protocol to abort any successful subtransaction from the unsuccessful aggregate transaction.

Timeliness in *CTP* is obtained from timeliness in *SP* and from the fact that the communication channels used by *CTP* in *AggregateAbort* sub-protocol are resilient.

3.5   Complex Transaction Protocol Providing Customer's Privacy

CTPCP uses as a building block the *Protocol including Physical Product Delivery that provides the Customer's Privacy* (*PPPDCP*) from Sect. 2.3 that involves physical products delivery for only one customer and one merchant.

CTPCP improves the protocol for complex transactions proposed in [5] with some important aspects. *CTPCP* uses *PPPDCP* that improves the protocol from [3] on which the solution from [5] is based. The details about these improvements were discussed in Sect. 2.3. This has two implications regarding *CTPCP*'s efficiency. First, *CTPCP* uses an offline TTP, while the protocol from [5] uses an online TTP. Second, the mechanism that provides customer's privacy in *CTPCP* is more efficient compared to how customer's privacy is obtained in [5]. Furthermore, these considerations lead to considering only two phases for *CTPCP*'s description, payment and delivery, while the protocol from [5] needs three protocol's phases: agreement, delivery, and payment. Also, *CTPCP* extends the complex transactions considered in [5] (that considers combinations of aggregate and optional transactions) taking into consideration partial transactions.

CTPCP is used when the customer wants to buy physical products in complex transactions from several merchants with preserving his privacy. *CTPCP* has the following participants: the customer C and his bank CB, the merchants M_i and their banks $M_i B$, the delivery agents DA_i, and the destination cabinets DC_i, where $1 \leq i \leq n$. We consider that all banks (CB and $M_i B$, where $1 \leq i \leq n$) share a commit-buffer and a list of currently used digital coins which will be used for the same purpose as in *PPPDCP*. Also, the capabilities of the destination cabinet from *PPPDCP* are extended to each DC_i in *CTPCP*.

The customer decides the products he wants to acquire, and as a result of the complex transaction he specifies in the online catalog, the customer's software builds the transaction tree t associated with the complex transaction. The transaction tree is defined as in Sect. 3.4.

We define *Payment* protocol consisting of *SPayment* sub-protocol from Sect. 2.3.1 and when necessary *Resolution 1* sub-protocol from Sect. 2.3.3.

A (payment) subtransaction s is denoted by $Payment(C', M_i, Pid_l)$ and is an instance of *Payment* protocol in which the customer buys from his bank a digital coin of corresponding value for acquiring the physical product with Pid_l identifier from the merchant M_i. Because the customer uses *Tor* anonymous network to communicate with M_i, he uses a different pseudo-identity C' in all communication with M_i.

We use the notations $Pe(s)$ and $Pe(s).Resp$, where $s = Payment(C', M_i, Pid_l)$, with the same meaning as in Sect. 3.4.

The state $St(p)$ of a node p is defined as in Definition 3.5, adapted to *CTPCP* with the following modification: if $p \rightarrow info = Pid_l$, then $St(p) = Pe(Payment(C', M_i, Pid_l))$.

CTPCP is described in Algorithm 3.2.1. *CTPCP* has the transaction tree t as input and searches a sequence of *PPPDCP*'s instances that meets the customer's options from t. Initially, the value λ is assigned to all node states in t (line 1).

In *CTPCP*, the execution of a *PPPDCP*'s instance in its entirety (from steps 1 until 9) is not an optimal solution. The reason for this is based on the possibility as in certain scenarios, the successful instances of *PPPDCP* (after *SDelivery* sub-protocol) must be aborted due to the fact that some other *PPPDCP*'s instances are aborted (after *SPayment* sub-protocol). Thus, to be more efficient, we require that the delivery of physical products is done only after the payment for these products is successfully realized. As a result, two phases are considered in *CTPCP*:

- *PayCTP* (Payment Complex Transactions Protocol)
- *DeliveryCTP* (Delivery Complex Transactions Protocol)

PayCTP(t) consists in applying *Payment* protocol to find a sequence of successful payment instances regarding the customer's options from t. After *PayCTP(t)* run (line 3), a sequence of payment evidences (*SPE*) is returned in which either all payment evidences are successful or all are aborted. *PayCTP(t)* is described in Algorithm 3.2.2, and we will provide explanations about it below.

DeliveryCTP(SPE) is applied when *PayCTP(t)* returns a *SPE* that contains only successful payment evidences. In this case (line 5), the delivery of each product from *SPE* is performed. *DeliveryCTP(SPE)* consists in applying *SDelivery* sub-protocol, and, when needed, *Resolution 2* and *3* sub-protocols from Sect. 2.3.3, for each product from *SPE*.

If after the execution of *DeliveryCTP(SPE)*, some *SDelivery*'s instances are aborted (due to the fact that C does not receive PRA or receives PRA but does not receive a product that is compliant with the corresponding PO), then the sequence of payment evidences *SPE1*, returned by *DeliveryCTP(SPE)*, contains successful and aborted payment evidences (obtained after *Resolution 2* or *3* sub-protocols). In this case, to maintain fairness, C initiates *SPE1Abort* sub-protocol (line 7), to abort all successful payment evidences from *SPE1*, by sending *SPE*, *SPE1*, and his signature on them to TTP. TTP requires to each merchant bank to abort his successful payment evidence from *SPE1*, in a similar manner with *Resolution 1* sub-protocol, case 2.

The product's identifiers from the subtransactions aborted (in *Resolution 2* or *3* sub-protocols) in *DeliveryCTP* are stored by TTP in an *AbortedPids* buffer and further used in *StoreAbortedStates(t)* procedure as follows:

$St(p) = \lambda$, for all nodes p in t, with $p \rightarrow info \in \{\vee, *, \wedge\}$ or $p \rightarrow info \notin$ *AbortedPids*.

In this way, all the node states that consist of aborted payment evidences obtained in *Resolution 2* or *3* sub-protocols are persistent in t for the next *CTPCP*'s round.

After a run of *CTPCP*, the customer's options may not be met, but these may not be fully explored. This case may occur because C's options have been analyzed in *PayCTP* (and were satisfied w.r.t. payment), but aborted in *DeliveryCTP*. So, *CTPCP* will search a new sequence of successful payment evidences to satisfy C's options by applying the two phases in multiple rounds. A round of *CTPCP* is applied

---

Algorithm 3.2.1 *CTPCP(t)*: complex transaction protocol providing customer's privacy

---

Input: Root t of the transaction tree associated with the complex transaction
Output: The sequence of payment evidences in which either all evidences are successful or all are aborted
1. $St(p) = \lambda$, for all nodes p in t;
2. **while** (1)
3. $SPE = PayCTP(t)$;
4.   **if** $(Pe(s).Resp = YES$, for all $Pe(s) \in SPE)$
5. $SPE1 = DeliveryCTP(SPE)$;
6.   **if** $(Pe(s).Resp = YES$, for all $Pe(s) \in SPE1)$ **return** *SPE1*;
7.   **else** *SPE1Abort*;
8.   *StoreAbortedStates(t)*; **end if**
9.   **else return** *SPE*; **end if**
10. **end while**

---

in a **while** loop iteration (lines 2–10), in which the products stored into *AbortedPids* buffer in all previous rounds are no longer taken into account. *CTPCP* terminates after a round that returns a successful payment evidence sequence that satisfies the customer's options (line 6) or after a round in which *PayCTP* returns an aborted payment evidence sequence (line 9).

Algorithm 3.2.2 describes *PayCTP*. It works in the same manner with Algorithm 3.1, with some modifications that will be described next. When *PayCTP* is applied in the first round of *CTPCP*, all the node states of t are λ. If *CTPCP* does not finish after the first round, then in t, there are some node states that consist of aborted payment evidences, and the other node states are λ. To ensure that the nodes which states consist of aborted payment evidences are not considered in the next *CTPCP*'s round, two tests are added in lines 1 and 7. *AggregateAbort(St(t))* sub-protocol is initiated by C by sending to TTP $St(t)$ and his signature on it, to abort any successful payment evidence from $St(p)$. TTP requires to each merchant bank to abort his successful payment evidence from $St(t)$, in a similar manner with *Resolution 1* sub-protocol, case 2.

3.5.1 CTPCP Security Discussion

Effectiveness of *CTPCP* is obtained from effectiveness of *PPPDCP*. If every party involved in *CTPCP* behaves honestly, then *CTPCP* is finished in a single round. Therefore, *CTPCP* applies only *SPayment* sub-protocol for each subtransaction in *PayCTP* and only *SDelivery* sub-protocol for each subtransaction in *DeliveryCTP*, without the involvement of TTP.

Algorithm 3.2.2 *PayCTP(t)*: payment complex transactions protocol

---

Input: Root t of the transaction associated with the complex transaction
Output: $St(t)$—State of t after payment
1. **if** $(t \to left \neq NULL$ and $St(t \to left) = \lambda)$ $child[0] = PayCTP(t \to left)$;
2. **if** $((t \to info = \vee$ and $Pe(s).Resp = YES$, for all $Pe(s) \in child[0])$ or
3. $\quad (t \to info = \wedge$ and $Pe(s).Resp = ABORT$, for all $Pe(s) \in child[0]))$
4. $\qquad St(t) = child[0]$; **return** $St(t)$;
5. $j = 1$; $k = t \to left \to right$;
6. **while** $(k \neq NULL)$
7. $\qquad$ **if** $(St(k) = \lambda)$ $child[j] = PayCTP(k)$;
8. $\qquad$ **if** $(t \to info = \vee$ and $Pe(s).Resp = YES$, for all $Pe(s) \in child[j])$
9. $\qquad\qquad St(t) = child[j]$; **return** $St(t)$;
10. $\qquad$ **if** $(t \to info = \wedge$ and $Pe(s).Resp = ABORT$, for all $Pe(s) \in child[j])$
11. $\qquad\qquad$ **for** $(c = 0; c \leq j; c = c + 1)$ $St(t) = St(t)child[c]$; **end for**
12. $\qquad\qquad AggregateAbort(St(t))$; **return** $ASt(t)$;
13. $\qquad k = k \to right$; $j = j + 1$;
14. **end while**
15. **if** $(t \to info = Pid_l)$ $St(t) = Pe(Payment(C', M_i, Pid_l))$; **return** $St(t)$;
16. **else if** $(t \to info = \vee)$
17. $\qquad k = t \to left$;
18. $\qquad$ **while** $(k \to right \neq NULL)$ $k = k \to right$; **end while**
19. $\qquad St(t) = St(k)$; **return** $St(t)$;
20. $\qquad$ **else if** $(t \to info = *)$
21. $\qquad\qquad$ **for** $(c = 0; c \leq j - 1; c = c + 1)$
22. $\qquad\qquad\qquad$ **if** $(Pe(s).Resp = YES$, for all $Pe(s) \in child[c])$
23. $\qquad\qquad\qquad\qquad St(t) = St(t)child[c]$; **end for**
24. $\qquad\qquad\qquad$ **if** $(c = j$ and $St(t) = \lambda)$ $St(t) = child[c - 1]$;
25. $\qquad\qquad\qquad$ **return** $St(t)$;
26. $\qquad\qquad$ **else for** $(c = 0; c \leq j - 1; c = c + 1)$ $St(t) = St(t)child[c]$; **end for**
27. $\qquad\qquad\qquad$ **return** $St(t)$;
28. $\qquad\qquad$ **end if**
29. $\qquad$ **end if**
30. **end if**

CTPCP assures strong fairness if after its execution, either C gets the sequence of physical products corresponding to his buying options and each M_i gets payment for the corresponding product or none do. Next, we analyze fairness in *CTPCP*, taking into account all scenarios in which C, M_i, DA_i, or DC_i behaves dishonestly. C can behave dishonestly only in *SPayment* sub-protocol from *Payment* protocol. So, all cases in which C behaves dishonestly were already discussed in Sect. 2.3.4. In all these cases, C receives from the corresponding merchant an aborted payment evidence. As a result of C's dishonest behavior, after *PayCTP* run, a sequence of aborted payment evidences is obtained, maintaining *CTPCP*'s fairness.

A merchant M_i can behave dishonestly in *SPayment* or *SDelivery* sub-protocols in scenarios discussed in Sect. 2.3.4. In all these cases, C and M_i receive an aborted payment evidence. Thus, if M_i behaves dishonestly in *SPayment*, then *CTPCP*'s fairness is maintained because, after *PayCTP* run, a sequence of aborted payment evidences is obtained. Otherwise, if M_i behaves dishonestly in *SDelivery*, then

SPE1Abort sub-protocol is applied to abort all successful payment evidences from the sequence *SPE1* obtained after *DeliveryCTP* run, ensuring fairness of *CTPCP*.

A delivery agent DA_i can behave dishonestly only in *SDelivery* sub-protocol, when he places a different product to DC_i's box than the one taken from M_i. This scenario is solved as in Sect. 2.3.4, both C and M_i receiving an aborted payment evidence after applying *Resolution 3* sub-protocol. Further, fairness of *CTPCP* is preserved by applying *SPE1Abort* sub-protocol.

A destination cabinet DC_i cannot behave dishonestly or be compromised by another party because DC_i has the same capabilities as DC from *PPPDCP*. As a result, *CTPCP* provides strong fairness.

Timeliness, non-repudiation, integrity, and confidentiality of *CTPCP* are direct consequences of the same security requirements provided by each *PPPDCP*'s instance.

Customer's privacy in *CTPCP* is obtained from customer's privacy in each instance of *PPPDCP* which is applied by *CTPCP*. The arguments for this are:

- The use of an electronic cash system based on blind digital signatures in each instance of *SPayment* sub-protocol which is applied in *PayCTP*. So, any party cannot make the connection between C and a digital coin bought by him.
- The communication between C and each merchant M_i is realized using *Tor* anonymous network. Consequently, the customer chooses a different pseudo-identity and a corresponding session public key in any subtransaction in which it is involved. Thus, no party or coalition between parties cannot link the real identity of the customer with his pseudo-identities used in *PPPDCP*'s instances or link different pseudo-identities used by the customer.
- The real identity of the customer is protected in *DeliveryCTP* by use of a destination cabinet DC_i with password-protected access.

In conclusion, *CTPCP* provides all the security requirements that *PPPDCP* provides.

3.6 Comparative Analysis

Table 3.1 presents a comparative analysis regarding the security requirements of the e-commerce protocols for physical products purchase which are used in multi-party scenarios. As we can see, the only solutions that can be used to buy physical products in complex transactions are those presented in Sect. 3.4 (what does not intend to obtain the customer's privacy) and Sect. 3.5 (in which the customer's privacy is guaranteed).

Table 3.1 Comparative analysis of multi-party e-commerce protocols

Protocols	CTP Sect. 3.4	CTPCP Sect. 3.5	Draper-Gil et al. [10]	Ferrer-Gomila et al. [11]
Scenario	Payment for physical products in complex transactions		Contract signing-different contracts	Contract signing-same contract
Atomicity	Yes	Yes	Yes	Yes
Effectiveness	Yes	Yes	Yes	Yes
Strong Fairness	Yes	Yes	No	Yes
Timeliness	Yes	Yes	Yes	Yes
Non-repudiation	Yes	Yes	Yes	Yes
Integrity	Yes	Yes	Yes	Yes
Confidentiality	Yes	Yes	Yes	Yes
Customer's Privacy	No	Yes	N.A.	N.A.

References

1. Asokan, N., Schunter, M., Waidner, M.: Optimistic Protocols for Multi-Party Fair Exchange. Technical Report IBM Research Report RZ 2892 (# 90840), IBM, Zurich Research Laboratory (1996)
2. Bao, F., Deng, R., Nguyen, K., Varadharajan, V.: Multi-party fair exchange with an off-line trusted neutral party. In: Tenth International Workshop on Database and Expert Systems Applications, pp. 858–862. IEEE, Piscataway (1999)
3. Bîrjoveanu, C.V.: Anonymity and fair-exchange in e-commerce protocol for physical products delivery. In: Proceedings of the 12th International Conference on Security and Cryptography—SECRYPT, (ICETE 2015), pp. 170–177. SCITEPRESS (2015). https://doi.org/10.5220/0005508801700177
4. Bîrjoveanu, C.V., Bîrjoveanu, M.: An optimistic fair exchange e-Commerce protocol for complex transactions. In: 15th International Joint Conference on e-Business and Telecommunications, ICETE 2018—vol. 2. SECRYPT, pp. 111–122. SCITEPRESS (2018). https://doi.org/10.5220/0006853502770288
5. Bîrjoveanu, C.V., Bîrjoveanu, M.: Preserving anonymity in fair exchange complex transactions e-commerce protocol for B2C/B2B applications. In: Proceedings of the 15th International Joint Conference on e-Business and Telecommunications, ICETE 2018, vol. 1, pp. 99–110. SCITEPRESS (2018). https://doi.org/10.5220/0006850802650276
6. Bîrjoveanu, C.V., Bîrjoveanu, M.: Automated verification of E-commerce protocols for complex transactions. In: Obaidat, M. (ed.) E-Business and Telecommunications. ICETE 2018. Communications in Computer and Information Science, vol. 1118, pp. 87–110. Springer, Cham (2019). https://doi.org/10.1007/978-3-030-34866-3_5
7. Bîrjoveanu, C.V., Bîrjoveanu, M.: Multi-party E-commerce protocol for B2C/B2B applications. In: Proceedings of the 16th International Joint Conference on e-Business and Telecommunications—ICE-B 2019, pp. 164–171. SCITEPRESS (2019). https://doi.org/10.5220/0007956801640171
8. Bîrjoveanu, C.V., Bîrjoveanu, M.: Anonymity in complex transactions for e-Business. In: Obaidat, M. (ed.) E-Business and Telecommunications. ICETE 2018. Communications in Computer and Information Science, vol. 1118. Springer, Cham (2019). https://doi.org/10.1007/978-3-030-34866-3_2

9. Cormen, T.H., Leiserson, C.E., Rivest, R.L., Stein, C.: Introduction to Algorithms, 3rd edn. MIT Press, Cambridge (2009)

10. Draper-Gil, G., Ferrer-Gomila, J.L., Hinarejos, M.F., Zhou, J.: An asynchronous optimistic protocol for atomic multi-two-party contract signing. Comput. J. **56**(10), 1258–1267 (2013)

11. Ferrer-Gomila, J.-L., Hinarejos, M.F.: A multi-party contract signing solution based on blockchain. Electronics **10**(12), 1457 (2021). https://doi.org/10.3390/electronics10121457

12. Franklin, M., Tsudik, G.: Secure group barter: multi-party fair exchange with semi-trusted neutral parties. In: Proceedings of Financial Cryptography 1998. Lecture Notes in Computer Science, vol. 1465, pp. 90–102. Springer, Berlin (1998)

13. González-Deleito, N., Markowitch, O.: An optimistic multi-party fair exchange protocol with reduced trust requirements. In: Kim, K. (ed.) Information Security and Cryptology—ICISC 2001. Lecture Notes in Computer Science, vol. 2288. Springer, Berlin, Heidelberg (2002). https://doi.org/10.1007/3-540-45861-1_20

14. Kılınç, H., Küpçü, A.: Optimally efficient multi-party fair exchange and fair secure multi-party computation. In: Nyberg, K. (ed.) Topics in Cryptology—CT-RSA 2015. Lecture Notes in Computer Science, vol. 9048. Springer, Cham (2015). https://doi.org/10.1007/978-3-319-16715-2_18

15. Liu, Y: An optimistic fair protocol for aggregate exchange. In: 2nd International Conference on Future Information Technology and Management Engineering, FITME 2009, pp. 564–567 (2009)

16. Mukhamedov, A., Ryan, M.D.: Fair multi-party contract signing using private contract signatures. Inform. Comput. **206**, 272–290 (2008)

17. Onieva, J.A., Lopez, J., Zhou, J.: Secure Multi-Party Non-Repudiation Protocols and Applications. Springer, Berlin (2009)

18. Onieva, J.A., Zhou, J., Carbonell, M., Lopez, J.: A multi-party non-repudiation protocol for exchange of different messages. In: Gritzalis, D., De Capitani di Vimercati, S., Samarati, P., Katsikas, S. (eds.) Security and Privacy in the Age of Uncertainty. SEC 2003. IFIP—The International Federation for Information Processing, vol. 122. Springer, Berlin (2003). https://doi.org/10.1007/978-0-387-35691-4_4

19. Zhou, J., Onieva, J., Lopez, J.: Optimized multi-party certified email protocols. Inform. Manag. Comput. Secur. **13**(5), 350–366 (2005). https://doi.org/10.1108/09685220510627250

Chapter 4
E-Commerce Protocols for Multi-chained Complex Transactions

4.1 State-of-the-Art Analysis

Currently, only a few solutions that consider intermediaries in different multi-party scenarios are proposed. Two solutions that consider an arbitrary number of intermediaries in scenarios which involves multiple parties are known: for buying physical products (Bîrjoveanu et al. [1]) and for digital contract signing (Draper-Gil et al. [3]). Multi-party protocols considering only one intermediary are proposed for buying digital/physical products (Carbonell et al. [2]) and for the exchange of non-repudiation evidences (Onieva et al. [5]).

In [5], Onieva et al. extend the multi-party protocol proposed in [4] to include an intermediary agent between the originator and many recipients. If we consider an e-commerce transaction, the originator is the customer which sends to the intermediary a request for buying digital products from many merchants. In this scenario, a merchant plays the role of recipient. The intermediary acts as a search agent sending the customer's request and the evidence of his involvement to the merchants. Some merchants respond with a corresponding reception evidence to the intermediary. Further, the intermediary sends to the customer the evidences received from merchants and also the evidence of his participation. Finally, in the same manner as in [4], only the corresponding merchants (which sent the response to the intermediary) will obtain the intended messages of the customer by communicating with *TTP*. Although the protocol provides a fair exchange of non-repudiation evidences between customer and intermediary, respectively, between intermediary and merchants, the payment method is not described. Similar with [4], the protocol ensures non-repudiation and timeliness but does not provide atomicity.

The solution proposed by Carbonell et al. [2] is based on the inclusion in the *3-D Secure Protocol* [6] of an intermediary agent who plays the role of a delegated agent, through which the customer can buy products from several providers. The model proposed by Carbonell et al. [2] adapts the Visa 3-D model by replacing the merchant and the acquirer from the acquirer domain by an intermediary agent and

© The Author(s), under exclusive license to Springer Nature Switzerland AG 2022
C. V. Bîrjoveanu, M. Bîrjoveanu, *Secure Multi-Party E-Commerce Protocols*,
SpringerBriefs in Computer Science, https://doi.org/10.1007/978-3-030-99351-1_4

his corresponding bank. Also, it considers many providers and their corresponding banks. The adapted *3-D Secure Protocol* is initiated by the customer who sends to the intermediary the purchase order and a public key certificate for the intermediary. This certificate is generated by the issuer in order to authorize the intermediary to send purchase requests only to the providers and for the products specified in the certificate. The intermediary has a *merchant plug-in* (*MPI*) installed with the same role as in *3-D Secure Protocol*. In the same way as in the *3-D Secure Protocol*, *MPI* sends to the *Access Control Server* (*ACS*) of the issuer via *Visa Directory Service* a request to determine whether the customer's card is enrolled in *Verified by Visa*. If the response from *ACS* specifies that the customer's card is enrolled, then *MPI* sends to *ACS* a customer authentication request in a similar manner with the *3-D Secure Protocol*. After the authentication procedure of the customer, *ACS* generates a signed response for each corresponding provider and sends it to *MPI*. After reception, *MPI* verifies the validity of all signed responses received from *ACS*, and if the customer's authentication is successful, then he sends each provider a purchase request that includes the products requested by the customer, the intermediary's certificate, and the corresponding signed response received from *ACS*. Each provider verifies the authenticity of the signed response (by checking *ACS*'s signature) and if the intermediary is authorized by the customer to send the purchase request (by checking the authenticity of the intermediary's certificate). If all these checks are successful, and if the customer has been successfully authenticated by *ACS*, then each provider sends a corresponding authorization request to his bank, which in turn sends it via *VisaNet* e-payment network to the issuer, in the same way as in *3-D Secure Protocol*.

This solution allows the customer to delegate an intermediary agent to facilitate the purchase of products from several providers and also the authentication and authorization of the customer during the online purchase. But, it does not provide the atomicity, even if the customer's authentication is done once for all the products that he wants to buy from several providers in the same transaction. This is because, in the authorization step of the same transaction, the issuer deals with each of the authorization requests individually. As a result, in the same transaction, the issuer may authorize the customer to purchase products from certain providers but does not authorize the customer to purchase other products from some providers (e.g., due to insufficient customer funds).

In [3], Draper-Gil et al. propose a multi-party contract signing protocol by involving many intermediaries between customer and providers. When the customer wants to purchase products, he sends a corresponding request to an intermediary, who in turn sends requests for the purchase of the products requested by the customer to one or more intermediaries or providers. The customer/an intermediary can request products from another intermediary/provider in two types of transactions: aggregate or partial. The protocol's goal is the fair exchange of digital signatures on contracts between the customer and intermediary and between the intermediary and another intermediary/provider. In a multi-party contract signing transaction, a chain of subtransactions is initiated, in which the customer/intermediary as the initiator of a subtransaction sends his commitment (his signature on the contract) to another intermediary/provider. If a provider agrees to the contract (commitment) received from an intermediary, then he sends him his acceptance (his signature on the contract). In order to send his own acceptance to the customer/intermediary from whom he received the commitment, each intermediary will have to obtain the acceptances from all the intermediaries/providers to which he sent his commitments. If the customer receives the appropriate acceptance from the intermediary, then he sends him an acknowledgment (his signature on acceptance) as proof of the agreement on the contract. Acknowledgments are propagated to all intermediaries/providers in the subtransaction chain, each intermediary sending its own acknowledgment to the intermediary/provider only after receiving the corresponding acknowledgment from the customer/intermediary to whom it sent the acceptance. If all parties involved behave honestly, then after the execution of the protocol, any two parties (customer-intermediary, intermediary-another intermediary, intermediary-provider) will obtain from each other the digital signature on the contract. If certain protocol's participants behave dishonestly, then to ensure fairness, two sub-protocols are used: *Cancel* and *Finish*. The *Cancel* sub-protocol is initiated by the customer/intermediary if, in a certain subtransaction, he does not receive a proper acceptance from the intermediary/provider to which he sent his commitment. Thus, the customer/intermediary sends a corresponding request to *TTP*, to which it responds depending on the status of the subtransaction. If the subtransaction has been finished, then *TTP* responds to the customer/intermediary with the corresponding acceptance and an acknowledgment signed by *TTP* as a proof of contract signing. If the subtransaction has been canceled or no subsequent subtransaction in chain has been finished, then *TTP* responds with a canceling evidence. An intermediary/provider initiates the *Finish* sub-protocol with *TTP* if, in a certain subtransaction, he does not receive a proper acknowledgment from the customer/intermediary to which he sent his acceptance. *TTP* responds either with a canceling evidence (if the subtransaction has been canceled) or with an acknowledgment signed by *TTP* (if no previous subtransaction in chain has been canceled). The protocol ensures effectiveness, weak fairness, timeliness, non-repudiation, and confidentiality.

In [1], the concept of *chained transaction* is defined for multi-party scenarios in which the customer wants to buy a physical product from a provider through several brokers.

In Sect. 4.4, we describe *Chained Transaction Protocol* (*ChainedTP*), which is an extension of the protocol for chained transaction proposed in [1]. This extension includes the interaction between the payment gateway on the one side and the customer bank and the bank of each broker on the other side.

A multi-party e-commerce protocol in which a customer wants to buy many physical products in complex transactions and each product is purchased in a chained transaction is proposed in [1]. These complex transactions are combinations in any form of aggregate and optional transactions.

In Sect. 4.5, we extend the solution from [1] in a *Multi-Chained Complex Transaction Protocol* (*MCCTP*) by considering combinations in any form of aggregate, optional, and partial transactions as complex transactions.

4.2   Applications B2C/B2B

Next, we provide application examples of *ChainedTP* and *MCCTP* for scenarios which include chained and complex transactions. We consider a firm Electron that produces electronic boards, and now it wants to construct a new test bench to test its new prototypes for the board. To construct this test bench, Electron will need several types of components: mounting rack, multi IO board, power supply, and connectors. To start the construction, Electron is browsing on the online catalog where he finds products from different big electronic parts seller Electronic Depot, Mounting System, Connects, and Acquisition Solutions. Electron needs a mounting rack preferably with the following dimensions 800 mm × 500 mm × 2000 mm (r1) from Mounting System, but if this is not possible, his second option for the rack is 600 mm × 600 mm × 2000 mm (r2) from Connects. It also needs a 14V power supply (pws) from Electronic Depot. For the test bench, Electron needs a multi IO board. The first option is a board with six analog inputs, four digital inputs, and four digital outputs (b1) from Acquisition Solutions. Its second option that will also fulfill its needs is a board with six analog inputs, six analog outputs, six digital inputs, and six digital outputs (b2) from Electronic Depot. To assemble the test bench, it needs a 24-pin right-angle connector (c1) from Mounting System and (because it has some back-up pieces left from the last constructed test bench) at least one of the following connectors (but is also satisfied if it will receive all connectors): 50-pin ribbon connector (c2) from Connects, 108-pin heavy duty connector (c3) from Connects, and 25-pin board mount connector (c4) from Connects.

To start the construction, Electron is browsing on the online catalog where he finds products from different merchants. He specifies his order in the form of a multi-chained complex transaction, as follows:

$$(r1 \lor r2) \land (pws) \land (b1 \lor b2) \land (c1 \land (c2 * c3 * c4))$$

Each individual product is acquired in a B2B chained transaction consisting of a chain of B2B subtransactions (exchanges). For example, the mounting rack r1 is acquired by Electron in a chained transaction (named chained$_1$) in which Mounting System is the intermediary. Thus, Electron initiates a subtransaction with Mounting System to buy r1. In his turn, to acquire r1, Mounting System initiates a new subtransaction with TechnicaHousingSolution, which is the producer/manufacturer of r1. Also, for example, to buy the power supply pws, Electron starts a chained transaction in which Electron Depot is the first broker, TestBenchSupply is the second broker, and PowerManufactor is the producer of pws.

The multi-chained complex transaction is successful if, for example, after Electron sends his order, it receives the pack, r1, pws, b2, c1, and c3, and each of them is successfully acquired in a chained transaction. The chained transaction chained$_1$ is successful if Electron receives a successful payment evidence from Mounting System and Mounting System receives payment from Electron and, respectively, Mounting System receives a successful payment evidence from

TechnicaHousingSolution and TechnicaHousingSolution receives payment from Mounting System.

The customer can be a person that likes electronics and builds electronic boards as a hobby and wants to test them. In this case, the multi-chained complex transaction is a complex transaction in which each chained transaction is a sequence of subtransactions B2C B2B . . . B2B.

4.3   Security Requirements

Strong fairness and security requirements closely related to strong fairness (effectiveness and timeliness) defined in the previous chapter for multi-party scenarios are not suitable for chained and multi-chained complex transactions. Next, we revise them for multi-party scenarios which include chained transactions, respectively, both chained and complex transactions.

Strong Fairness in Chained Transaction Protocol. *ChainedTP* ensures strong fairness if after its execution, either the chained transaction is successfully completed, meaning that each party that initiates an exchange in the chained transaction (the customer or a broker) receives the successful payment evidence from the corresponding merchant (broker or provider) and each receiver broker or provider receives the payment for the product from the corresponding initiator, or none of the involved parties receives nothing.

Strong Fairness in Multi-chained Complex Transaction Protocol. *MCCTP* ensures strong fairness if after its execution, the following statements are fulfilled:

- *ChainedTP* ensures strong fairness in every chained transaction from the complex transaction, and
- For any optional transaction from the complex transaction, either there is exactly one successful chained transaction (corresponding to an option), or in all chained transactions (all options), no party receives anything, and
- For any aggregate transaction from the complex transaction, either all the chained transactions are successful, or in all chained transactions, no party receives anything, and
- For any partial transaction from the complex transaction, either at least one of the chained transactions is successfully completed, or in all chained transactions no party receives anything.

Effectiveness requires that if every party involved in *ChainedTP* (*MCCTP*) behaves honestly and no communication error occurs, then after protocol execution, the chained transaction (all chained transactions) is (are) successfully completed without *TTP* mediation.

Timeliness in *ChainedTP* (*MCCTP*) is defined in a similar manner as in the previous chapter, but regarding the above strong fairness requirements.

We enhance *confidentiality* in chained transactions to include another business requirement with respect to the identities of participants. Thus, we require that in any chained transaction from *ChainedTP* or *MCCTP*, each party knows only the identities of the parties with whom he/she communicates. This requirement is important because if in a chained transaction a broker learns the identity of the provider with whom he does not make any exchange, then in the next chained transaction, the broker can address directly to the provider, excluding the other brokers.

4.4   Chained Transaction Protocol

In real-world e-commerce transactions, there are scenarios in which the customer wants to buy a physical product from a broker, who must in his turn buy the product from another broker or provider, and then sell it to the customer. This type of transaction is named *chained transaction*, in which the customer buys a physical product from a broker using a provider and possibly several other brokers. The provider from a chained transaction is the party who produces the physical product. Each broker involved in the chained transaction buys the product from another broker or provider and sells it to the customer or another broker that requests it. Examples of these scenarios can be found in Sect. 4.2.

In a chained transaction, certain issues may arise regarding fairness. For example, in a chained transaction, a broker B_2 can buy the physical product, but he cannot sell it to the broker B_1 who requested it. This scenario can happen when B_1's account balance is not enough to allow him to buy the product he ordered to B_2. In such a scenario, fairness is not provided, because B_2 remains with a product he has nothing to do with. As a result, there is a need for solutions that provide fairness in chained transactions to ensure a business model in which all parties involved can trust to use it.

ChainedTP we describe has the following participants: the customer, the brokers, the provider, the payment gateway, the customer bank, and the bank of each broker. Table 4.1 presents the notations used in the description of *ChainedTP*. In Table 4.1, we use extensions of the notations from Table 2.2 Chap. 2 used to describe *SP*. In *ChainedTP*, we consider the same assumptions as in *SP* regarding the types of communications channels used between involved parties. Also, the customer and each broker have a payment Web segment software with the same goal as in *SP*. Because in *ChainedTP* several banks are involved, we extend the assumptions regarding public key certificates from *SP* such that only the payment gateway has the authentic public key certificates for all banks involved. The other assumptions from *SP* regarding digital certificates are extended to each broker from the chain. We consider that a trusted authority issues a provider certificate $CertP_j$, for each provider P_j, where $1 \leq j \leq k$, to certify P_j as a provider for a specific physical product manufactured by P_j.

Table 4.1 Notations used in *ChainedTP* description

Notation	Interpretation
C, PG, P_j	Identity of Customer, Payment Gateway, Provider j, where $1 \leq j \leq k$
B_i	Identity of Broker i, where $1 \leq i \leq n$. If $i = 0$, then B_i denotes C.
	If $i = n$, then B_{i+1} denotes one of the providers $P_1, \ldots, P_k$, and $E_{i+1} = CertB_{n+1}$.
$B_i B$	Identity of Broker i Bank, where $1 \leq i \leq n$
$PO_{i,i+1}$	Purchase Order of B_i to B_{i+1}: $\{PM_i, OI_i\}_{PkB_{i+1}}$
PM_i	Payment Message of B_i: $\{PI_i, SigB_i(PI_i)\}_{PkPG}$
PI_i	Payment Information of B_i: $B_i, Cn_i, Otp_i, Id_i, Am_i, PkB_i, B_{i+1}$
s_i	Subtransaction in which B_i buys the product with Pid identifier from B_{i+1}
Id_i	Identifier of the subtransaction s_i: $Id_{i-1}N_i$
	If $i = 0$, then Id_{i-1} is the empty string.
OI_i	Order Information of B_i to B_{i+1}:
	$B_i, B_{i+1}, Pid, Id_i, Am_i, PkB_i, SigB_i(B_i, B_{i+1}, Pid, Id_i, Am_i, PkB_i)$
$PR_{i,i+1}$	Payment Request of B_{i+1} to B_i:
	$\{PM_i, B_{i+1(ac)}, SigB_{i+1}(Id_i, B_i, B_{i+1}, PkB_i, Am_i, B_{i+1(ac)})\}_{PkPG}$
$PAR_{i,i+1}$	Payment Authorization Request in s_i:
	$\{PI_i, B_{i+1(ac)}, SigPG(PI_i, B_{i+1(ac)})\}_{PkB_i B}$
$PA_{i,i+1}$	Payment Acknowledgment in s_i:
	$Resp, B_i, B_{i+1}, Id_i, SigB_i B(Resp, B_i, B_{i+1}, Id_i, Am_i)$
$PE_{i,i+1}$	Payment Evidence of B_i and B_{i+1} in s_i:
	$Resp, B_i, B_{i+1}, Id_i, SigPG(Resp, B_i, B_{i+1}, Id_i, Am_i), E_i$
E_i	Payment Evidence in s_i that B_i sends to B_{i-1}: $Resp, Id_i, SigPG(Resp, Id_i)$
$PE_{i,i+1}.Resp$	The response $Resp$ in $PE_{i,i+1}$
$E_i.Resp$	The response $Resp$ in E_i

The *Chained Transaction Protocol* in which the customer C wants to buy the physical product with Pid identifier from the broker B_j using many other brokers and a provider, denoted by *ChainedTP(C, B_j, Pid)*, is described in Algorithm 4.1. After *ChainedTP*'s execution, a sequence of subtransactions $s_0 s_1 \ldots s_n$ that defines the chained transaction is carried out. In each subtransaction s_i, where $0 \leq i \leq n$, B_i buys the physical product with Pid identifier from B_{i+1}. The number n represents the number of brokers involved in the chained transaction, B_0 denotes C, and B_{n+1} denotes one of the providers $P_1, \ldots, P_k$. Figure 4.1 graphically represents the *ChainedTP*'s messages.

Initially (the first line of Algorithm 4.1), we rename the broker j's identity, B_j, in the identity of the broker 1, B_1, to make easier the notational tracking of the flow of messages between the parties involved in *ChainedTP(C, B_j, Pid)*.

In **while** loop (lines 2–5), $n + 1$ subtransactions $s_0, s_1, \ldots, s_n$ are started. These subtransactions belong to the chained transaction $s_0 s_1 \ldots s_n$. In the first iteration of the **while** loop, C initiates *ChainedTP* by initiating the first subtransaction s_0 from the chain. For this, C generates a fresh random number N_0 that will be used

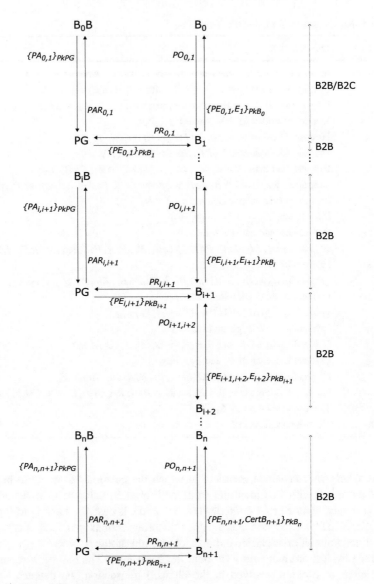

Fig. 4.1 *ChainedTP*'s messages

as a unique identifier Id_0 for s_0. C sends the purchase order $PO_{0,1}$ to the broker B_1 for buying the physical product with Pid identifier. In turn, to complete the request received from C, B_1 initiates the next subtransaction s_1 from the chain by generating a fresh random number N_1 that will be used to compute the identifier Id_1 of s_1 as being the sequence consisting of s_0's identifier $Id_0 = N_0$ and N_1. Then, B_1 sends to B_2 the purchase order $PO_{1,2}$ to acquire the physical product with Pid identifier. Similarly, in the ith iteration of **while** loop, B_i generates a fresh random number N_i necessary to compute the identifier Id_i of s_i as being the sequence of all numbers $N_0 N_1 \ldots N_i$ generated in all subtransactions $s_0, s_1, \ldots, s_i$. B_i initiates the subtransaction s_i to purchase from B_{i+1} the product requested by B_{i-1} in s_{i-1}. If a request $PO_{i,i+1}$ reaches the corresponding provider, then the **while** loop is finished, and the last subtransaction from the chained transaction was initiated. The last subtransaction is s_n, and the provider is B_{n+1}. The subtransaction's identifiers are associated in such a way as to allow later the easy establishment of the subtransaction's execution order in the chained transaction. This is very important in situations in which solving of a later dispute is necessary.

Algorithm 4.1 *ChainedTP(C, B_j, Pid)*: chained transaction protocol

---

Input: The customer C that wants to buy the physical product with Pid identifier from the broker B_j using many other brokers and a provider
Output: A chained transaction as a sequence of subtransactions $s_0 s_1 \ldots s_n$ in which either all subtransactions are successful or all are aborted
1. $B_1 = B_j$; $i = 0$;
2. **while** $(B_i \notin \{P_1, \ldots, P_k\})$
3. $B_i \rightarrow B_{i+1} : PO_{i,i+1}$
4. $i = i + 1$;
5. **end while**
6. $n + 1 = i$;
7. $B_{n+1} \rightarrow PG : PR_{n,n+1}$
8. $PG \rightarrow B_n B : PAR_{n,n+1}$
9. $B_n B \rightarrow PG : \{PA_{n,n+1}\}_{PkPG}$
10. $PG \rightarrow B_{n+1} : \{PE_{n,n+1}\}_{PkB_{n+1}}$
11. $B_{n+1} \rightarrow B_n : \{PE_{n,n+1}, CertB_{n+1}\}_{PkB_n}$
12. **for** $(i = n - 1; i \leq 0; i = i - 1)$
13.   **if** $(B_{i+2} \rightarrow B_{i+1} : \{PE_{i+1,i+2}, E_{i+2}\}_{PkB_{i+1}}$ in s_{i+1},
14.   with $PE_{i+1,i+2}.Resp = YES$ and $E_{i+2}.Resp = YES$)
15. $B_{i+1} \rightarrow PG : PR_{i,i+1}$
16. $PG \rightarrow B_i B : PAR_{i,i+1}$
17. $B_i B \rightarrow PG : \{PA_{i,i+1}\}_{PkPG}$
18. $PG \rightarrow B_{i+1} : \{PE_{i,i+1}\}_{PkB_{i+1}}$
19.   **if** $(PE_{i,i+1}.Resp = YES)$ $B_{i+1} \rightarrow B_i : \{PE_{i,i+1}, E_{i+1}\}_{PkB_i}$
20.   **else** *Resolution 1(B_{i+1})*; **break**;
21.   **end if**
22.   **else if** $(B_{i+2} \rightarrow B_{i+1} : \{PE_{i+1,i+2}\}_{PkB_{i+1}}$ in s_{i+1},
23.   with $PE_{i+1,i+2}.Resp = ABORT$) *Resolution 1($B_{i+2}$)*; **break**;
24.   **else** *Resolution 2(B_{i+1})*; **break**;
25.   **end if**
26.   **end if**
27. **end for**

A chained transaction $s_0 s_1 \ldots s_n$ is successful after *ChainedTP* execution if all subtransactions s_i, where $0 \leq i \leq n$, are successful. This means that for all subtransactions s_i, where $0 \leq i \leq n$, B_i receives the successful payment evidence $PE_{i,i+1}$ in s_i and successful payment evidence E_{i+1} in s_{i+1} and B_{i+1} receives the payment for the corresponding product, meaning the successful $PE_{i,i+1}$. To ensure fairness in a chained transaction, any subtransaction s_i is successful only after the successful completion of the next subtransactions $s_{i+1}, s_{i+2}, \ldots, s_n$. Therefore, we require that for any subtransaction s_i, B_i must receive two successful payment evidences: $PE_{i,i+1}$ that ensures B_i that s_i is successful and also E_{i+1} that provides B_i a proof of successful of s_{i+1}. A chained transaction $s_0 s_1 \ldots s_n$ is aborted after *ChainedTP* execution if all subtransactions s_i, where $0 \leq i \leq n$, are aborted. This means that for all s_i, where $0 \leq i \leq n$, B_i and B_{i+1} receive an aborted $PE_{i,i+1}$.

The completion of the chained transaction is achieved by completing its component subtransactions in the reverse order to the order in which these were initiated. Thus, Algorithm 4.1 completes the subtransactions from the chained transaction $s_0 s_1 \ldots s_n$ beginning with the completion of s_n, then s_{n-1}, and so on until s_0. The message flow corresponding to the subtransaction s_n is described at lines 7–11. Upon receiving $PO_{n,n+1}$ from B_n and successfully checking it, the provider B_{n+1} sends the payment request $PR_{n,n+1}$ to PG for obtaining the payment from B_n. If $PR_{n,n+1}$'s verification by PG is successful, then he sends the payment authorization request $PAR_{n,n+1}$ to B_n's bank B_nB. B_n's authorization for using the card is checked by B_nB, and if it is successful, then it sends a payment acknowledgment $PA_{n,n+1}$ to PG, which in turn sends to B_{n+1} a successful $PE_{n,n+1}$. Otherwise, if some check fails, then B_nB sends an abort message to PG, which in turn sends to B_{n+1} an aborted $PE_{n,n+1}$. The payment evidence $PE_{n,n+1}$ in s_n extends the payment evidence PE from Table 2.2 used in SP, by adding a new payment evidence component E_n that will be used in the subtransaction s_{n-1} by B_n to inform B_{n-1} about the success or abortion of s_n. The evidence E_i added in the payment evidence $PE_{i,i+1}$ of each subtransaction s_i ensures that all subtransactions from the chained transaction will have the same response (*YES* or *ABORT*). After B_{n+1} verifies the authenticity of $PE_{n,n+1}$, he sends it to B_n, together with his provider certificate $CertB_n$. B_n checks also the authenticity of $PE_{n,n+1}$ and $CertB_n$.

After the completion of the subtransaction s_n, the **for** loop continues performing the subtractions s_{n-1}, s_{n-2}, and so on, until s_0, each iteration performing s_i depending on the success or abortion of s_{i+1}, where $n - 1 \geq i \geq 0$.

In what follows, we describe the iteration of **for** loop in which the subtransaction s_i is performed, where $n - 1 \geq i \geq 0$, after the subtransactions $s_n, s_{n-1}, \ldots, s_{i+1}$ have already been completed in this order.

The broker B_{i+1} is involved in the subtransactions s_i and s_{i+1} from the chained transaction. In the subtransaction s_{i+1}, B_{i+1} is the buyer from B_{i+2} of the product requested to him by B_i, while in the subtransaction s_i, B_{i+1} is the seller of the product (acquired from B_{i+2}) to B_i. B_{i+1} responds to the request received in s_i from B_i, depending on the success of all subtransactions $s_{i+1}, s_{i+2}, \ldots, s_n$ or abortion of all of them. So, if in s_{i+1}, B_{i+1} receives from B_{i+2} a successful $PE_{i+1,i+2}$ and a successful E_{i+2} (lines 13–14), then B_{i+1} is ensured that all subtransactions

$s_{i+1}, s_{i+2}, \ldots, s_n$ were successfully completed. In this case, B_{i+1} sends $PR_{i,i+1}$ to PG in the subtransaction s_i. After sending the messages corresponding to the subtraction s_i from lines 16 to 18, upon receiving a successful $PE_{i,i+1}$, B_{i+1} sends $PE_{i,i+1}$ and E_{i+1} to B_i (line 19). B_i checks if the received evidences are authentic, fresh, and successful and belong to successive subtransactions by verifying their corresponding identifiers. If all checks are successfully passed, then the success of the evidences ensures B_i that s_i and s_{i+1} were successfully completed. If B_{i+1} receives from PG an aborted $PE_{i,i+1}$, then the subtransaction s_i is aborted, and subsequently, the entire chained transaction must be aborted. Thus, B_{i+1} initiates *Resolution 1* sub-protocol (line 20) described in Sect. 4.4.1.

If B_{i+1} receives from B_{i+2} an aborted $PE_{i+1,i+2}$, then the subtransaction s_{i+1} is aborted, and also, in this case, B_{i+2} initiates *Resolution 1* sub-protocol (line 23) to abort the entire chained transaction. If B_{i+1} receives from B_{i+2} a successful $PE_{i+1,i+2}$, but E_{i+2} is missing or aborted, then even if B_{i+1} is ensured that the subtransaction s_{i+1} is successful, he has no guarantees that the subtransactions $s_{i+2}, s_{i+3}, \ldots, s_n$ are successful. In this case, B_{i+1} initiates the *Resolution 2* sub-protocol (line 24) either to get a successful E_{i+2} or to abort the entire chained transaction. Section 4.4.2 describes the *Resolution 2* sub-protocol.

4.4.1 Resolution 1 Sub-protocol

Regarding fairness in *ChainedTP*, the following scenario requires special attention: $s_0 s_1 \ldots s_n$ is a chained transaction in which for $0 \leq i < n$, the subtransactions $s_{i+1}, s_{i+2}, \ldots, s_n$ are successful, but the subtransaction s_i is aborted because B_{i+1} receives in s_i an aborted $PE_{i,i+1}$ from PG. In this case, fairness in *ChainedTP* is not ensured because the entire chained transaction is aborted, but some of its subtransactions are successful. To provide fairness, *Resolution 1* sub-protocol is initiated by B_{i+1} to abort all subtransactions from the chained transaction. Algorithm 4.1.1 describes *Resolution 1* sub-protocol. In the **if** instruction, the algorithm aborts the successful subtransaction s_{i+1}, based on the fact that s_i is aborted. B_{i+1} requests to PG the abortion of s_{i+1}, by sending it the aborted $PE_{i,i+1}$ and the successful $PE_{i+1,i+2}$. In turn, PG sends the request to B_{i+1}'s bank. After $B_{i+1}B$ successfully verifies the evidence's authenticity and if they belong to the successive subtransactions from the chain, he cancels the transfer corresponding to s_{i+1}, generates an aborted acknowledgment payment evidence $AAPE_{i+1,i+2}$ for $PE_{i+1,i+2}$, and sends it to PG. $AAPE_{i+1,i+2}$ is calculated by $B_{i+1}B$ as follows:

$$AAPE_{i+1,i+2} = ABORT, B_{i+1}, B_{i+2}, Id_{i+1},$$

$$SigB_{i+1}B(ABORT, B_{i+1}, B_{i+2}, Id_{i+1}, Am_{i+1}, PE_{i+1,i+2}), AAE_{i+1},$$

where $AAE_{i+1} = ABORT, Id_{i+1}, SigB_{i+1}B(ABORT, Id_{i+1}, E_{i+1})$.

Algorithm 4.1.1 *Resolution 1(B_{i+1})*: *Resolution 1* sub-protocol

---

Input: A chained transaction $s_0 s_1 \ldots s_n$ in which s_i, where $0 \leq i \leq n$, is the first aborted subtransaction in the order from s_n to s_0
Output: An aborted chained transaction
if $(i < n)$ $B_{i+1} \rightarrow PG : \{PE_{i,i+1}, PE_{i+1,i+2}\}_{PkPG}$
$\qquad\qquad PG \rightarrow B_{i+1}B : \{PE_{i,i+1}, PE_{i+1,i+2}\}_{PkB_{i+1}B}$
$\qquad\qquad B_{i+1}B \rightarrow PG : \{AAPE_{i+1,i+2}\}_{PkPG}$
$\qquad\qquad PG \rightarrow B_{i+1} : \{APE_{i+1,i+2}\}_{PkB_{i+1}}$
$\qquad\qquad PG \rightarrow B_{i+2} : \{APE_{i+1,i+2}\}_{PkB_{i+2}}$
end if
for $(j = i + 2; j \leq n; j = j + 1)$
$\qquad B_j \rightarrow PG : \{APE_{j-1,j}, PE_{j,j+1}\}_{PkPG}$
$\qquad PG \rightarrow B_jB : \{APE_{j-1,j}, PE_{j,j+1}\}_{PkB_jB}$
$\qquad B_jB \rightarrow PG : \{AAPE_{j,j+1}\}_{PkPG}$
$\qquad PG \rightarrow B_j : \{APE_{j,j+1}\}_{PkB_j}$
$\qquad PG \rightarrow B_{j+1} : \{APE_{j,j+1}\}_{PkB_{j+1}}$
end for
$B_{i+1} \rightarrow B_i : \{PE_{i,i+1}\}_{PkB_i}$
for $(j = i; j \geq 1; j = j - 1)$
$\qquad B_j \rightarrow PG : \{PE_{j,j+1}, PM_{j-1}, OI_{j-1}\}_{PkPG}$
$\qquad PG \rightarrow B_j : \{PE_{j-1,j}\}_{PkB_j}$
$\qquad PG \rightarrow B_{j-1} : \{PE_{j-1,j}\}_{PkB_{j-1}}$
end for

PG checks the authenticity of $AAPE_{i+1,i+2}$, and if it is successfully passed, he computes the aborted $PE_{i+1,i+2}$, denoted by $APE_{i+1,i+2}$, as follows:

$$APE_{i+1,i+2} = ABORT, B_{i+1}, B_{i+2}, Id_{i+1},$$

$$SigPG(ABORT, B_{i+1}, B_{i+2}, Id_{i+1}, Am_{i+1}, PE_{i+1,i+2}), AE_{i+1},$$

where $AE_{i+1} = ABORT, Id_{i+1}, SigPG(ABORT, Id_{i+1}, E_{i+1})$.

Then, PG sends the aborted payment evidence $APE_{i+1,i+2}$ to B_{i+1} and B_{i+2}. As a result, s_{i+1} became aborted.

The first **for** loop aborts the subtransactions $s_{i+2}, s_{i+3}, \ldots, s_n$ in a similar way as above. Each **for** loop iteration aborts a subtransaction s_j, where $i + 2 \leq j \leq n$, using the fact that the subtransaction s_{j-1} has already been aborted in a previous **for** loop iteration (with a single exception in which s_{i+1} has already been aborted in the **if** instruction).

After B_{i+1} sends the aborted $PE_{i,i+1}$ to B_i, the second **for** loop aborts $s_{i-1}, s_{i-2} \ldots, s_0$ in this order. Each iteration of the second **for** loop aborts a subtransaction s_{j-1}, where $i \leq j \leq 1$, in which B_j sends a corresponding request to PG that contains the payment message PM_{j-1} and the order information OI_{j-1} received by him in s_{j-1} and the aborted $PE_{j,j+1}$. On successful authenticity verification of $PM_{j-1}, OI_{j-1}, PE_{j,j+1}$, and their belongingness to the successive subtransactions, PG generates an aborted evidence $PE_{j-1,j}$ and sends it to B_j and B_{j-1}. As a result, s_{j-1} is aborted.

4.4.2 Resolution 2 Sub-protocol

For a subtransaction s_{i+1} from the chained transaction $s_0 s_1 \ldots s_n$, in which B_{i+1} sends $PO_{i+1,i+2}$ to B_{i+2}, the following scenarios are not preserving fairness in *ChainedTP*:

- B_{i+1} does not receive from B_{i+2} any valid payment evidences $PE_{i+1,i+2}$ and E_{i+2}.
- B_{i+1} receives from B_{i+2} a successful $PE_{i+1,i+2}$ in s_{i+1}, but E_{i+2} from s_{i+2} is aborted or missing.

To restore fairness, *Resolution 2* sub-protocol is applied at line 24 of *ChainedTP*. So, a timeout interval is considered in each subtransaction s_{i+1} from the chained transaction, in which B_{i+1} waits the payment evidences from B_{i+2}. If B_{i+1} does not receive the corresponding payment evidences from B_{i+2} and the timeout interval is passed, then *Resolution 2* sub-protocol is initiated by B_{i+1} to receive either both successful $PE_{i+1,i+2}$ and E_{i+2} or the aborted $PE_{i+1,i+2}/APE_{i+1,i+2}$. To request the corresponding evidence from s_{i+1}, B_{i+1} sends $\{PM_{i+1}, OI_{i+1}\}_{PkPG}$ to PG. After checking the validity of B_{i+1}'s request, PG checks its database searching for $PE_{i+1,i+2}$. The following situations can be encountered:

1. If PG finds both $PE_{i+1,i+2}$ and E_{i+2} successful, then PG sends them to B_{i+1}, and *ChainedTP* goes further with s_i.
2. If PG finds the successful $PE_{i+1,i+2}$, but E_{i+2} is aborted or not founded, then PG communicates with $B_{i+1}B$ to generate $APE_{i+1,i+2}$. To confirm the abortion of s_{i+1} to B_{i+1} and B_{i+2}, PG sends them $APE_{i+1,i+2}$. Next, B_{i+2} initiates *Resolution 1* to abort $s_{i+2}, \ldots, s_n$ if these are successful, and also B_{i+1} initiates *Resolution 1* to abort $s_i, \ldots, s_0$.
3. If PG finds the aborted $PE_{i+1,i+2}$, then he sends it to B_{i+1} and B_{i+2} to ensure them of s_{i+1} abortion. Therefore, *Resolution 1* is applied as in case 2.
4. If PG does not find $PE_{i+1,i+2}$, then PG generates the aborted evidence $PE_{i+1,i+2}$ and sends it to B_{i+1} and B_{i+2}. *Resolution 1* is applied as in case 2.

ChainedTP Security Discussion

ChainedTP ensures effectiveness, strong fairness, timeliness, non-repudiation, integrity, and confidentiality. Strong fairness, non-repudiation, integrity, and confidentiality are formally proved in Chap. 5 using AVISPA for the case that considers one broker in a chained transaction.

4.5   Multi-chained Complex Transactions Protocol

In Sect. 3.4, we presented a multi-party e-commerce protocol that is used in scenarios in which a customer wants to buy physical products in complex transactions from many merchants. Further, in Sect. 4.4, we described a solution that allows a customer to buy a physical product from a broker in a chained transaction in which many other brokers and one provider can be involved. Starting from the business models that include complex transactions and chained transactions independently, we naturally extend them to a business model which takes into consideration both complex and chained transactions. This combined business model considers scenarios in that a customer wants to buy many physical products in complex transactions, in which each product is purchased in a chained transaction.

MCCTP is based on *Complex Transaction Protocol* from Algorithm 3.1, Chap. 3, adapted to scenarios in which the customer purchases each physical product (from complex transaction) in a chained transaction. Thus, *MCCTP* extends the scenarios from *CTP* in which the customer may purchase each physical product (from complex transaction) only in a subtransaction.

Definition 4.1   A chained transaction ct, denoted by $ChainedTP(C, B_j, Pid_l)$, is an instance of *ChainedTP* in which the customer C buys from the broker B_j the physical product with Pid_l identifier, using many other brokers and one provider.

Definition 4.2   For a chained transaction $ct = ChainedTP(C, B_j, Pid_l)$, the payment evidence $Pe(ct)$ corresponding to ct is the payment evidence $PE_{0,j}$ that C will receive in ct.

$Pe(ct)$ emphasizes the abortion or success of the chained transaction ct.

The state $St(p)$ of a node p is defined extending Definition 3.5, Chap. 3, to chained transactions. So, $St(p)$ is the sequence of the payment evidences $Pe(ct_1) \ldots Pe(ct_m)$ corresponding to the chained transactions $ct_1 \ldots ct_m$ initiated by C for buying the product defined by p. $St(p)$ is calculated in the same manner as in Definition 3.5, with the following modifications:

- If $p \rightarrow info = Pid_l$, then $St(p) = Pe(ChainedTP(C, B_j, Pid_l))$.
- If $p \rightarrow info \in \{\vee, *, \wedge\}$, then the payment evidence $Pe(s)$ corresponding to a subtransaction s is replaced by $Pe(ct)$ corresponding to a chained transaction ct, and the expression "*subtransaction(s)*" is replaced by "*chained transaction(s)*".

MCCTP is described by an algorithm that works similarly with Algorithm 3.1, adapted to chained transactions, as follows:

- *CTP* from header and lines 1 and 7 is replaced by *MCCTP*.
- $Pe(s)$ in replaced by $Pe(ct)$, where ct is a chained transaction.
- Line 12 is modified replacing $AggregateAbort(St(t))$ with the $AggregateChainsAbort(St(t))$ sub-protocol that is described below.
- At line 15, $Pe(SP(C, M_i, Pid_l))$ is replaced by $Pe(ChainedTP(C, B_j, Pid_l))$.

4.5.1 AggregateChainsAbort Sub-protocol

The *AggregateChainsAbort* sub-protocol is applied in *MCCTP* if the fairness for the customer is not ensured. Such a situation may arise when for a node p corresponding to $\wedge$ operator, $St(p)$ is the payment evidence's sequence of the form:

$$St(p) = Pe(ChainedTP(C, B_1, Pid_1)) \ldots Pe(ChainedTP(C, B_m, Pid_m)),$$

such that, for any $1 \leq i \leq k < m$, $Pe(ChainedTP(C, B_i, Pid_i)) = PE_{0,i}$ is successful and, for any $k + 1 \leq j \leq m$, $Pe(ChainedTP(C, B_j, Pid_j)) = PE_{0,j}$ is aborted. In this case, the aggregate product $(Pid_1, \ldots, Pid_m)$ is not successfully purchased, even if the component products $Pid_1, \ldots, Pid_k$ are successfully purchased in the chained transactions $ChainedTP(C, B_i, Pid_i)$, where $1 \leq i \leq k < m$.

Algorithm 4.2.2 describes the *AggregateChainsAbort* sub-protocol that is applied to restore fairness for cases like the one mentioned above. The first four messages and the first **for** loop from Algorithm 4.2.2 are similar to the messages in *AggregateAbort* sub-protocol from Sect. 3.4.1, but in Algorithm 4.2.2, the node state $St(p)$ contains the payment evidences of chained transactions. Also, CB generates $AASt(p)$, respectively, PG generates $ASt(p)$ as in *Resolution 1* sub-protocol from Algorithm 4.1.1. After the transmission of the first four messages and of the messages from the first **for** loop, the aborted payment evidences $APE_{0,1}, \ldots, APE_{0,k}$ are generated. These aborted evidences correspond to the abortion of the first

---

Algorithm 4.2.2 *AggregateChainsAbort($St(p)$): AggregateChainsAbort* sub-protocol

---

Input: $St(p)$ for a node p corresponding to $\wedge$ operator, of the form $St(p) = Pe(ChainedTP(C, B_1, Pid_1)) \ldots Pe(ChainedTP(C, B_m, Pid_m))$, such that, for any $1 \leq i \leq k < m$, $Pe(ChainedTP(C, B_i, Pid_i))$ is successful and, for any $k + 1 \leq j \leq m$, $Pe(ChainedTP(C, B_j, Pid_j))$ is aborted; the number n_i of brokers involved in any chained transaction $ChainedTP(C, B_i, Pid_i)$, where $1 \leq i \leq k$

Output: $ASt(p)$—the aborted $St(p)$, and $ChainedTP(C, B_i, Pid_i)$ is aborted, where $1 \leq i \leq m$

$C \rightarrow PG : \{St(p), SigC(St(p))\}_{PkPG}$
$PG \rightarrow CB : \{St(p)\}_{PkCB}$
$CB \rightarrow PG : \{AASt(p)\}_{PkPG}$
$PG \rightarrow C : \{ASt(p) = APE_{0,1}, \ldots, APE_{0,k}\}_{PkC}$
for $(i = 1; i \leq k; i = i + 1)$
$\quad PG \rightarrow B_i : \{APE_{0,i}\}_{PkB_i}$
end for
for $(i = 1; i \leq k; i = i + 1)$
$\quad$ **for** $(j = i; j \leq n_i; j = j + 1)$
$\quad\quad B_j \rightarrow PG : \{APE_{0,j}, PE_{j,j+1}\}_{PkPG}$
$\quad\quad PG \rightarrow B_jB : \{APE_{0,j}, PE_{j,j+1}\}_{PkB_jB}$
$\quad\quad B_jB \rightarrow PG : \{AAPE_{j,j+1}\}_{PkPG}$
$\quad\quad PG \rightarrow B_j : \{APE_{j,j+1}\}_{PkB_j}$
$\quad\quad PG \rightarrow B_{j+1} : \{APE_{j,j+1}\}_{PkB_{j+1}}$
$\quad$ **end for**
end for

subtransaction of each successful chained transaction $ChainedTP(C, B_i, Pid_i)$),
where $1 \leq i \leq k$.

The second **for** loop aborts the chained transactions $ChainedTP(C, B_i, Pid_i)$),
where $1 \leq i \leq k$. Each iteration aborts the chained transaction $ChainedTP(C, B_i, Pid_i)$) in an inner **for** loop in a similar manner as in *Resolution 1*, using the fact that
the first subtransaction of $ChainedTP(C, B_i, Pid_i)$) has been already aborted.

MCCTP Security Discussion

MCCTP is based on *ChainedTP*. As a result, the way *MCCTP* is designed
ensures its effectiveness, strong fairness, timeliness, non-repudiation, integrity, and
confidentiality.

References

1. Bîrjoveanu, C.V., Bîrjoveanu, M.: Fair exchange E-commerce protocol for multi-chained complex transactions. In: 17th International Joint Conference on e-Business and Telecommunications—Volume 2: ICE-B, pp. 49–60. SCITEPRESS (2020). https://doi.org/10.5220/0009824000490060
2. Carbonell, M., Maria Sierra, J., Lopez, J.: Secure multiparty payment with an intermediary entity. Comput. Secur. **28**, 289–300 (2009)
3. Draper-Gil, G., Zhou, J., Ferrer-Gomila, J.L., Hinarejos, M.F.: An optimistic fair exchange protocol with active intermediaries. Int. J. Inform. Secur. **12**, 299–318 (2013). https://doi.org/10.1007/s10207-013-0194-9
4. Onieva, J.A., Zhou, J., Carbonell, M., Lopez, J.: A multi-party non-repudiation protocol for exchange of different messages. In: Gritzalis, D., De Capitani di Vimercati, S., Samarati, P., Katsikas, S. (eds.) Security and Privacy in the Age of Uncertainty. SEC 2003. IFIP—The International Federation for Information Processing, vol. 122. Springer, Berlin (2003). https://doi.org/10.1007/978-0-387-35691-4_4
5. Onieva, J.A., Zhou, J., Lopez, J., Carbonell, M.: Agent-mediated non-repudiation protocols. Electron. Commerce Res. Appl. **3**, 152–162 (2004)
6. Visa: Verified by Visa Acquirer and Merchant Implementation Guide (2011). https://usa.visa.com/dam/VCOM/download/merchants/verified-by-visa-acquirer-merchant-implementation-guide.pdf. Cited June 25, 2022

Chapter 5
Formal Verification of Multi-party Fair Exchange E-Commerce Protocols

5.1 AVISPA Tool

The tools for the automatic verification of security protocols based on formal methods of analysis are focused on model checking [22, 25], theorem proving [21], and hybrid techniques [13]. The most representative automatic tools for security protocol verification are AVISPA [1], Casper/FDR [19], and ProVerif [8] for model checking; Isabelle/HOL [6] for theorem proving; and Scyther [12] and Tamarin [20] for hybrid techniques.

We will use the *Automated Validation of Internet Security Protocols and Applications* (*AVISPA*) tool to formally verify the multi-party e-commerce protocols detailed in Chap. 4. The AVISPA tool was developed as a joint work between the Information Security group (ETH), the CASSIS group (INRIA), the Artificial Intelligence Laboratory (DIST), and Siemens AG. AVISPA is widely used by academic researchers, as well as by designers of industry-scale security protocols [16, 25]. The verification using AVISPA on Internet Engineering Task Force (IETF) security protocols found attacks on some of them [25].

AVISPA uses the *High-Level Protocol Specification Language* (*HLPSL*) [3, 4, 10] to specify a protocol, security properties, and the scenario to analyze. HLPSL is a modular language based on Temporal Logic of Actions in [17]. The input of AVISPA is a HLPSL specification which is automatically translated, using the *HLPSL2IF* translator, into a low-level specification—the *Intermediate Format* (*IF*). An IF specification [3] uses rewriting rules to model a protocol as an infinite-state transition system, being suitable as input for the back-ends of the AVISPA tool.

Four back-ends that implement different approaches to verifying security protocols are integrated into the AVISPA tool: *Constraint-Logic-based Attack Searcher* (*CL-AtSe*), *On-the-Fly Model-Checker* (*OFMC*), *SAT-based Model-Checker* (*SAT MC*), and *Tree Automata-based Protocol Analyzer* (*TA4SP*).

CL-AtSe [24] analyzes a bounded number of protocol's sessions, in which the search for attacks is correct and complete. It translates an IF specification of a security protocol into a set of constraints which is used to find attacks on the security protocol. The technique implemented by CL-AtSe models each protocol's step through a set of constraints relative to the intruder's knowledge. Thus, a message received by an honest participant is a constraint for it to be sent by the intruder, because the intruder is considered the environment through which communication between honest agents takes place. CL-AtSe reduces the number of protocol's steps to be analyzed by merging as many steps together as possible and by eliminating protocol's execution branches which are unnecessary. The verification is done using both options: typed and untyped model. The *typed model* option is set by default, considering that all variables and constants are typed. The *untyped model* option ignores all type information by considering all variables to be of generic type *message*, being an option used for the detection of type-flaw attacks. Also, CL-AtSe supports the XOR operator and most properties of the exponentiation.

OFMC [5] analyzes a bounded number of protocol's sessions without bounding the messages an intruder can generate. It builds a tree representation corresponding to the security protocol's execution, using a number of symbolic techniques to represent the state space. OFMC implements the XOR operator and exponentiation and analyzes both typed and untyped model options.

SATMC [2] reduces the problem of verifying the correctness of a security protocol to the SAT problem. It encodes an IF specification of a security protocol through a propositional formula, which is provided to a SAT solver. Finally, any model found is translated back into an attack on the security protocol. SATMC analyzes a bounded number of protocol's sessions, considering only typed model.

TA4SP [9] approximates the intruder knowledge by using tree automata and rewriting. It provides results for analyzing of unbounded number of protocol's sessions.

All AVISPA back-ends consider a Dolev-Yao intruder [14] that controls the communication channels under the *perfect cryptography assumption*. In this assumption, all cryptographic primitives are perfect, meaning that the intruder can decrypt an encrypted message only if he has the appropriate decryption key and can encrypt a message only if he has the appropriate encryption key. The Dolev-Yao intruder fully controls the network, so it can intercept any message, block further transmission, decompose messages using known keys, generate fresh data as needed, compose new messages from known data and send, impersonate any honest agent, or play roles in the protocol like any other participant in the protocol.

5.1.1   High-Level Protocol Specification Language

We will describe *High-Level Protocol Specification Language* (*HLPSL*) using as an example a security protocol for *authenticated session key distribution* (*ASKD*) between a client C and a service provider P by using an authentication server S. We consider a scenario similar to the one from the Kerberos protocol [11] in which the agents registered in the system have long-term symmetric keys shared with the

Table 5.1 *ASKD* protocol

1. $C \rightarrow P : C, P, N_c, \{C, P, N_c\}_{K_{cs}}$
2. $P \rightarrow S : C, P, N_c, \{C, P, N_c\}_{K_{cs}}, N_p, \{C, P, N_c\}_{K_{ps}}$
3. $S \rightarrow P : N_c, \{N_c, N_p, K_{cp}\}_{K_{cs}}, \{N_p, K_{cp}\}_{K_{ps}}$
4. $P \rightarrow C : N_c, \{N_c, N_p, K_{cp}\}_{K_{cs}}, \{N_c, N_p\}_{K_{cp}}$
5. $C \rightarrow P : N_c, \{N_p, N_c\}_{K_{cp}}$

server S. An agent's long-term key is generated by the hash of the password with which the agent is registered. Thus, C has the long-term symmetric key K_{cs} shared with S, while P shares with S the long-term symmetric key K_{ps}. The idea of the protocol is that C and P use S to establish a private communication channel between them whenever they need it. Once the private channel is established between C and P, the access of client C to the service provided by P is made secure, without the intervention of S.

The *ASKD* protocol's messages are described in Table 5.1. The protocol's goals are establishing a session key K_{cp} between C and P, and mutual authentication between C and P, without the use of timestamps. Thus, the protocol does not require the synchronization of participant's clocks as in the Kerberos protocol. The client C initiates the *ASKD* protocol by sending to the service provider P a request to access his service. For this, C generates a unique random number N_c and sends it to P both cleartext and encrypted with his long-term key K_{cs}. On reception, P generates in turn a unique random number N_p and sends to S, in message 2, a request for a session key that will encrypt its subsequent communication with C. This request contains the request received by P from C, the number N_p, and the encryption of C, P, and N_c with P's long-term key K_{ps}. S decrypts the encrypted components of message 2 and checks if C, P, and N_c received in cleartext and in the encrypted components are the same. If this check is successful, then S is assured that P has sent C's request without any modification. As a result, S generates a new session key K_{cp} and sends it to P in two certificates: $\{N_c, N_p, K_{cp}\}_{K_{cs}}$ for C and $\{N_p, K_{cp}\}_{K_{ps}}$ for P. The presence of the numbers generated by C/P in certificates intended for C/P is essential to ensure the freshness of the session key K_{cp}. On the reception of message 3, P decrypts his certificate, obtains K_{cp}, and verifies if the number received in certificate matches with the number generated by him in the request sent to S in message 2. The successful verification ensures P that K_{cp} is a new session key intended for communication with C. Therefore, P forwards to C the certificate intended for him, together with a message encrypted with K_{cp} ($\{N_c, N_p\}_{K_{cp}}$), to confirm to C the knowledge of the session key K_{cp}. In the same way as P, C checks the freshness of the received session key, by checking if the number received in his certificate matches the one generated by him in the request from message 1. If the session key is new, then C uses it to decrypt the second part of message 3. Then, if after decryption the numbers obtained match with those from his certificate, then he confirms the knowledge of K_{cp} by sending message 5 to P. P makes the same checks as C on the reception of message 5. After protocol execution, C and P share a new authenticated session key K_{cp}, each of them having the confirmation that the other knows K_{cp}. As a result, C can securely access the service from P, K_{cp} being used by both to encrypt/decrypt all subsequent traffic between them.

The question is whether this conclusion regarding $ASKD$ protocol's goals, obtained through informal arguments, can be obtained also after the formal verification of his requirements. To answer this question, we model $ASKD$ protocol in $HLPSL$ to verify the protocol's goals using the AVISPA model checkers.

Usually, the security protocols are described as sequences of communication steps, using the *standard notation*, as in Table 5.1. As we can see, the standard notation describes only the exchange of messages between protocol's participants in the intended behavior of the protocol, under normal conditions. Thus, this notation is a high-level, intuitive description and cannot describe accurately the behavior of a complex, large-scale protocol that runs in a real environment. To model the complex protocols, we need a language that provides more expressiveness, allowing constructions like *if then else* and *loops*. While there are specification languages more closed to the standard notation [19, 22], we will use an expressive language: *HLPSL*.

Specifying a protocol in *HLPSL* is modular and consists of specifying:

1. The role of each agent in protocol.
2. The protocol's session by composing the roles of the agents in protocol.
3. The execution environment and the protocol scenario to be verified.
4. The security properties to analyze.
5. The scenario execution.

Messages and Types

The *atomic messages* consist of agent names, fresh random generated numbers (nonces), numbers, symmetric and public keys, hash functions, labels, and communication channels. The *messages* are generated from the atomic messages using the following functions: concatenation ($M.N$ denotes concatenation of the messages M and N), encryption (M_K denotes the encryption of the message M using the key K), and hashing ($H(M)$ denotes the application of the hash function H on the message M).

The parameters, variables, and constants used in a protocol specification are typed. For the atomic messages, the following types are used: `agent` for agent names, `text` for fresh generated numbers, `nat` for numbers, `symmetric_key` for symmetric keys, `public_key` for public keys, `hash_func` for hash functions, `protocol_id` for labels, and `channel(dy)` for communication channels considering a Dolev-Yao intruder. A special type named *message* is used to represent an arbitrary message.

Agent Roles

In *ASKD* protocol, three roles are identified, played by the client, service provider, and authentication server. For each of the three roles, a corresponding *agent role* (or *basic role*) is specified in *HLPSL*, as we can see below. An agent role specifies its *parameters*, *local variables* by the `local` keyword, *constants* by the `const` keyword, *initial state* by the `init` keyword, and *transitions* by the `transition` keyword.

The parameters of the `client` role are the agent names from *ASKD* protocol (`C, P, S` of type `agent`), the key `Kcs` (of type `symmetric_key`) shared between `C` and `S`, and the communication channels `Snd` and `Rcv` (of type `channel(dy)`) through which the agent `C` playing the `client` role will communicate. The local variables of the `client` role are a natural number `State` for representing the role's state; the random numbers `Nc` and `Np` generated by `C` and `P`, respectively; and the new session key `Kcp`. In the initial state, the variable `State` is initialized to `0`.

The client's behavior in the *ASKD* protocol is described by the two transitions of the `client` role. Usually, a precondition defines the conditions necessary for the application of a transition. If the precondition is satisfied, then the transition's effect is described by performing a certain action. The first transition of the `client` role models the transmission of message 1 from *ASKD* protocol (Table 5.1). The precondition of this transition is satisfied if the value of `State` is `0` and the protocol's session `start` signal is received by the client on `Rcv` channel. To build the first message, the client uses the `new()` function to generate a new random number `Nc`. We remark the use of `Nc'` (and not `Nc`) to represent the new value of the variable `Nc`. The action of this transition sets the new value of `State` to `1`, sends the first protocol message on `Snd` channel, and specifies a *witness* goal fact. The goal facts will be described later in a dedicated paragraph.

In what follows, we will explain the transitions from the client, provider, and server roles in an intercalated manner, to accurately capture how the agents playing the client, provider, and server roles communicate with each other to achieve the protocol's goal.

The reception by the provider of the first message from the protocol and the sending of message 2 to the server are modeled by the first transition of the `provider` role. Thus, if the `provider` role's state is `0` and he receives from the customer the message `C.P.Nc'.X'` on `Rcv` channel, then the new value of the role's state is `1`, and the provider generates his random number `Np` and sends message 2 of the protocol on `Snd` channel. The first two components of the message `C.P.Nc'.X'` require the transition to be applied only if the first two components match the current values of the variables `C` and `P`, respectively. The provider expects to receive in the third component a random number generated by the customer. For this, `Nc'` is used with the meaning that the provider assigns to `Nc` the value received on the third component of the message. The last component of the message is an encrypted component with a key unknown to the provider, so the provider cannot decrypt it. Therefore, this component is modeled by `X'`, where `X` is the variable of a compound type {agent.agent.text}_symmetric_key corresponding to the expected component type.

Agent roles communicate with each other through communication channels. For example, the client sends the message C.P.Nc'.{C.P.Nc'}_Kcs on the Snd channel, and the provider receives it on the Rcv channel. The connection between the two channels is made by the Dolev-Yao intruder who is considered the network. Thus, any message sent by an honest agent arrives to the intruder, and any message received by an honest agent comes from the intruder. In this way, the intruder's non-deterministic behavior is modeled: the intruder can observe, modify, or block a transmitted message if the message received on Rcv channel matches, differs, or is missing from the message sent on Snd channel.

The server role has only one transition that models message 2 reception by the server from the provider and sending of message 3 to the provider. The second transition of the provider role models the reception of message 3 and sending of message 4 to the client, while the corresponding reception by the client and the sending of message 5 to the provider are modeled by the second transition of the client role. The reception of the last *ASKD* protocol's message is specified in the third transition of the provider role.

```
role client(C,P,S: agent, Kcs: symmetric_key,
            Snd,Rcv: channel(dy)) played_by C def=

local
  State: nat,
  Nc,Np: text,
  Kcp: symmetric_key

init
  State := 0

transition

1. State = 0 /\ Rcv(start) =|>
   State':= 1 /\ Nc' := new() /\ Snd(C.P.Nc'.{C.P.Nc'}_Kcs)
   /\ witness(C,P,p_c_nc,Nc')

2. State = 1 /\ Rcv(Nc.{Nc.Np'.Kcp'}_Kcs.{Nc.Np'}_Kcp') =|>
   State':= 2 /\ Snd(Nc.{Np'.Nc}_Kcp')
   /\ request(C,P,c_p_np,Np')

end role

role provider(C,P,S: agent, Kps: symmetric_key,
              Snd,Rcv: channel(dy)) played_by P def=

local
  State: nat,
  Np,Nc: text,
  Kcp: symmetric_key,
  X: {agent.agent.text}_symmetric_key,
```

```
    Y: {text.text.symmetric_key}_symmetric_key

init
  State := 0

transition

1. State = 0 /\ Rcv(C.P.Nc'.X') =|>
   State':=1/\ Np':=new()/\ Snd(C.P.Nc'.X'.Np'.{C.P.Nc'}_Kps)

2. State = 1 /\ Rcv(Nc.Y'.{Np.Kcp'}_Kps) =|>
   State':= 2 /\ Snd(Nc.Y'.{Nc.Np}_Kcp')
   /\ witness(P,C,c_p_np,Np)

3. State = 2 /\ Rcv(Nc.{Np.Nc}_Kcp) =|>
   State':= 3 /\ request(P,C,p_c_nc,Nc)

end role

role server(C,P,S: agent, Kcs,Kps: symmetric_key,
        Snd,Rcv: channel(dy)) played_by S def=

local
  State: nat,
  Nc,Np: text,
  Kcp: symmetric_key

init
  State := 0

transition

1.State= 0/\ Rcv(C.P.Nc'.{C.P.Nc'}_Kcs.Np'.{C.P.Nc'}_Kps) =|>
  State'  := 1 /\ Kcp'  := new()
  /\ Snd(Nc'.{Nc'.Np'.Kcp'}_Kcs.{Np'.Kcp'}_Kps)
  /\ secret(Kcp',skcp,{C,P,S})

end role
```

Composed Roles

The *composed roles* have no transitions, being defined by parallel composition (specified by the /\ operator) of several roles using the composition keyword. The protocol's session and the protocol scenario we want to analyze are modeled as composed roles. The session role from below describes a *ASKD* protocol's session by parallel composition (interleaving) the client, provider, and server agent roles.

```
role session(C,P,S: agent, Kcs,Kps: symmetric_key) def=

local
  Snd,Rcv: channel (dy)

composition
  client(C,P,S,Kcs,Snd,Rcv)
  /\ provider(C,P,S,Kps,Snd,Rcv)
  /\ server(C,P,S,Kcs,Kps,Snd,Rcv)

end role
```

The environment role presented below specifies the constants, the initial intruder's knowledge, and the protocol scenario to be analyzed. Initially, the intruder knows the identity of the client (c), provider (p), and server (s) and the symmetric key kis shared between him and the server. The parallel composition of three protocol's sessions defines the protocol scenario, where the first session is played between honest agents, and in the second and third sessions, the intruder (i) plays the provider and the customer role, respectively.

```
role environment() def=

const
  c,p,s: agent,
  kcs,kps,kis: symmetric_key,
  c_p_np, p_c_nc, skcp: protocol_id

intruder_knowledge = {c,p,s,kis}

composition
  session(c,p,s,kcs,kps)
  /\ session(c,i,s,kcs,kis)
  /\ session(i,p,s,kis,kps)

end role
```

Security Properties

AVISPA provides support for the specification of confidentiality and two forms of authentication: strong and weak. For the *ASKD* protocol, the security properties we require are the confidentiality of the session key Kcp and the strong mutual authentication between the client and provider. These security properties are described below, in the goal section.

The confidentiality of the session key Kcp is specified using the secrecy_of keyword by secrecy_of skcp, where the constant skcp of protocol_id type (declared in the `environment` role) identifies the goal. The `skcp` identifier is used in a goal fact `secret(Kcp', skcp,{C,P,S})` that is added to the action of the transition from the `server` role that generates `Kcp`. This goal fact requires the session key `Kcp` to be a secret shared between the client, service provider, and server.

To specify the strong mutual authentication between the client and service provider, we need to specify the strong authentication of the client to the service provider on the value `Nc` and the strong authentication of the service provider to the client on the value `Np`. The strong authentication of the client to the service provider on `Nc` is specified using the `authentication_on` keyword by `authentication_on p_c_nc`, where `p_c_nc` is a constant of `protocol_id` type that identifies the goal. The `p_c_nc` identifier is used in two goal facts in the roles involved in strong authentication, as follows:

- The goal fact `witness(C,P,p_c_nc,Nc')` is added in the first transition of the `client` role, to specify that the client `C` wants to authenticate itself to the service provider `P` on the value `Nc` generated by him.
- The goal fact `request(P,C,p_c_nc,Nc)` is added in the last transition of the `provider` role (when `C` proves to `P` that he can encrypt `Np.Nc` with the new session key), to specify that `P` accepts the authentication of `C` being ensured that `Nc` was indeed created by `C`.

The *ASKD* protocol ensures strong authentication of the client to the service provider on `Nc`, if for a goal fact `request`, a unique corresponding `witness` was previously emitted with the first agent names reversed, the same identifier `p_c_nc`, and the same instance of `Nc`. The strong authentication corresponds to the (injective) agreement from [18].

Also, we use the `c_p_np` identifier to specify the strong authentication of the service provider to the client on the value `Np`. Regarding this, a `witness` goal fact is added in the second transition of the provider role and a corresponding `request` in the last transition of the `client` role.

```
goal
  secrecy_of skcp
  authentication_on p_c_nc
  authentication_on c_p_np
end goal
```

If we want to model a weak form of authentication that does not guarantee one-to-one correspondence between sessions (in contrast to the strong authentication), then we use the `weak_authentication` keyword in the `goal` section and `witness` and `wrequest` goal facts in the corresponding roles. The weak authentication corresponds to the non-injective agreement from [18], in which for many `wrequest` facts, only a `witness` can be used.

The scenario execution specified in the `environment` role is performed by calling `environment()`.

5.1.2   Verification Results Using AVISPA

To verify the *HLPSL* specification of *ASKD* protocol, we use SPAN (Security Protocol Animator) from [23]. SPAN provides a graphical interface that allows to build the Message Sequence Charts as representations of the execution of a *HLPSL* specification. Three options are available to be used in SPAN [15]: *Protocol Simulation*, *Intruder Simulation*, and *Attack Simulation*.

The *Protocol Simulation* option builds a Message Sequence Chart (MSC) corresponding to the *ASKD* protocol's execution in which only the honest agents are considered (client, service provider, and server). Figure 5.1 shows MSC for the *ASKD* protocol using *Protocol Simulation* option, in a form closer to standard notation, in which the intruder is not considered. This option is useful to check if the *HLPSL* specification of the *ASKD* protocol is correct. As we can see, the *ASKD* protocol's message exchange in Fig. 5.1 is complete, meaning that the specification is correct.

The *Intruder Simulation* option allows building of MSCs corresponding to the executions of the *ASKD* protocol taking into consideration the intruder. This option offers the ability to manually build attacks on a security protocol or to rebuild a known attack on a security protocol.

AVISPA back-ends return only the first attack found, without being able to find attacks on many security goals in a single check. So, we verify the security goals one by one. The results of the *ASKD* protocol verification using CL-AtSe and OFMC back-ends show that the protocol is safe regarding confidentiality and unsafe regarding both authentication goals. SATMC and TA4SP back-ends do not support the *ASKD* protocol verification. The *Attack Simulation* option allows to view as MSCs the attacks on the *ASKD* protocol found by CL-AtSe and OFMC back-ends. The output generated by CL-AtSe, presented below, proves that an authentication attack on `(p,c,p_c_nc,Nc(5))` has been found, providing a trace of attack leading to violation of the `authentication_on p_c_nc` goal. Figure 5.2 shows MSC generated using the *Attack Simulation* option, which corresponds to the attack trace found by CL-AtSe.

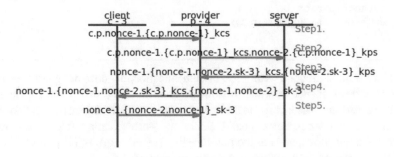

Fig. 5.1 *ASKD* protocol simulation in SPAN

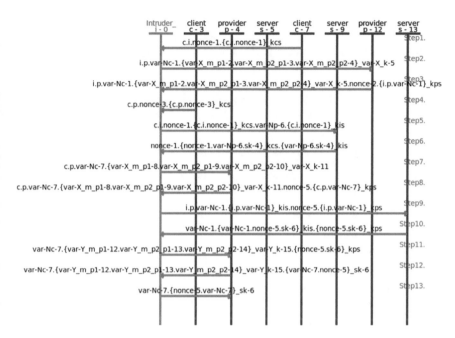

Fig. 5.2 *ASKD* attack simulation in SPAN

```
SUMMARY        UNSAFE

DETAILS        ATTACK_FOUND
               TYPED_MODEL
PROTOCOL       /home/span/span/testsuite/results/ASKD.if
GOAL           Authentication attack on (p,c,p_c_nc,Nc(5))
BACKEND        CL-AtSe
STATISTICS     Analysed  : 883 states
               Reachable : 614 states
               Translation: 0.01 seconds
               Computation: 0.60 seconds
ATTACK TRACE
i -> (c,7): start
(c,7) -> i: c.i.n13(Nc).{c.i.n13(Nc)}_kcs


i -> (p,12): i.p.Nc(25).{X_m_p1(19).X_m_p2_p1(19).X_m_p2_p2(19)}_X_k(19)
(p,12) -> i: i.p.Nc(25).{X_m_p1(19).X_m_p2_p1(19).X_m_p2_p2(19)}_X_k(19)
             .n19(Np).{i.p.Nc(25)}_kps


i -> (c,3): start
(c,3) -> i: c.p.n1(Nc).{c.p.n1(Nc)}_kcs & Witness(c,p,p_c_nc,n1(Nc));

i -> (s,9): c.i.n13(Nc).{c.i.n13(Nc)}_kcs.Np(17).{c.i.n13(Nc)}_kis
(s,9) -> i: n13(Nc).{n13(Nc).Np(17).n17(Kcp)}_kcs.{Np(17).n17(Kcp)}_kis
             & Secret(n17(Kcp),set_92); Add c to set_92; Add i to set_92;
             & Add s to set_92;
```

```
i -> (p,4): c.p.Nc(5).{X_m_p1(5).X_m_p2_p1(5).X_m_p2_p2(5)}_X_k(5)
(p,4) -> i: c.p.Nc(5).{X_m_p1(5).X_m_p2_p1(5).X_m_p2_p2(5)}_X_k(5).
            n5(Np).{c.p.Nc(5)}_kps

i -> (s,13): i.p.Nc(25).{i.p.Nc(25)}_kis.n5(Np).{i.p.Nc(25)}_kps
(s,13) -> i: Nc(25).{Nc(25).n5(Np).n25(Kcp)}_kis.{n5(Np).n25(Kcp)}_kps
             & Secret(n25(Kcp),set_95); Add i to set_95;
             Add p to set_95; & Add s to set_95;

i -> (p,4): Nc(5).{Y_m_p1(6).Y_m_p2_p1(6).Y_m_p2_p2(6)}_Y_k(6).
            {n5(Np).n25(Kcp)}_kps
(p,4) -> i: Nc(5).{Y_m_p1(6).Y_m_p2_p1(6).Y_m_p2_p2(6)}_Y_k(6).
            {Nc(5).n5(Np)}_n25(Kcp) & Witness(p,c,c_p_np,n5(Np));

i -> (p,4): Nc(5).{n5(Np).Nc(5)}_n25(Kcp)
(p,4) -> i: () & Request(p,c,p_c_nc,Nc(5));
```

In the following, we analyze the *ASKD* protocol's attack trace generated by CL-AtSe, in order to understand why the attack is found and to identify the error in the protocol that allows it. The attack begins with the intruder i sending the start signal to initiate a protocol's session with the client c. (c, 7) denotes the instance of the client role identified by the number 7. The client (c, 7) responds to i with a message corresponding to the first step of the protocol, in which (c, 7) wants to access a service from i. The notation n13 (Nc) is used to represent the new value generated for Nc. The intruder continues this protocol's session by sending to the provider role's instance (p, 12) a message in which he wants to access a service from (p, 12). The new value created by i for Nc is denoted by Nc (25), and the variable X_ is used as a component which cannot be checked by i. The provider (p, 12) responds to i with a message corresponding to the second step of the protocol.

Next, i initiates a second protocol's session with the client (c, 3), who responds to him with a message corresponding to the first step of the protocol, in which (c, 3) wants to access a service from the provider p. As we can see, the intruder is the intermediary for all messages exchanged between agents, because he is considered the network. We remark that in this step, a Witness (c, p, p_c_nc, n1 (Nc)) goal fact is generated, meaning that c wants to authenticate p using the value n1 (Nc). The intruder continues this protocol's session by sending to the provider (p, 4) a message corresponding to the first protocol's step, but including his own number Nc (5), and not the number n1 (Nc) generated by (c, 3).

```
i -> (p,4): c.p.Nc(5).{X_m_p1(5).X_m_p2_p1(5).X_m_p2_p2(5)}_X_k(5)
```

After i receives the response from (p, 4), he learns the number n5 (Np) generated by (p, 4) for a shared key with the client.

```
(p,4) -> i: c.p.Nc(5).{X_m_p1(5).X_m_p2_p1(5).X_m_p2_p2(5)}_X_k(5).
            n5(Np).{c.p.Nc(5)}_kps
```

Further, i sends to the `server` role's instance (`s,13`) a request for obtaining a session key shared between him and the provider using `Nc(25)` as his number and `n5(Np)` as the number generated by the provider (`p,4`). Then, the intruder sends to the provider (`p,4`) the certificate received for him from the server (`s,13`) that includes a session key `n25(Kcp)`. The provider (`p,4`) accepts `n25(Kcp)` as a valid session key for communication with the client, because the certificate containing it includes the number `n5(Np)` generated by (`p,4`) for such a key. Moreover, i can confirm the knowledge of the session key `n25(Kcp)` to (`p,4`) in the last message. As a result, the provider accepts the authentication of the client on the value `Nc(5)`, generating `Request(p,c,p_c_nc,Nc(5))`, while there is no previous witness corresponding to this request (the previous `Witness(c,p,p_c_nc,n1(Nc))` is not corresponding).

Formal verification using AVISPA shows that the *ASKD* protocol has some flaws because it does not provide all the security properties for which it was designed. The main issue is to extract essential information from the attack provided by CL-AtSe to help us design a safe protocol. The cause of the attack is that although the numbers generated by the client and provider must be included by the server in the certificates they receive, these numbers are not a substitute for the identity of the agent with whom the session key in the certificate is shared. This is because these numbers are not sent to the server in a protected way and can be changed by the intruder. As a result, the goal of using the random numbers for binding a received certificate to a sent request is lost: a session key from a certificate received by an agent including the number previously generated by him in a corresponding request may not be dedicated to communicating with the desired agent. Thus, each certificate must include the identity of the agent with whom the session key is shared, in addition to the session key and the previously generated number.

According to the above arguments, we propose a new variant of protocol, called *ASKDFixed* protocol, which is obtained modifying *ASKD* protocol by including the service provider identity in the client's certificate and the client identity in the service provider's certificate. Thus, the only changes compared to the *ASKD* protocol are in messages 3 and 4 (messages 1, 2, and 5 are the same) as follows:

3. $S \to P : N_c, \{P, N_c, N_p, K_{cp}\}_{K_{cs}}, \{C, N_p, K_{cp}\}_{K_{ps}}$
4. $P \to C : N_c, \{P, N_c, N_p, K_{cp}\}_{K_{cs}}, \{N_c, N_p\}_{K_{cp}}$

The verification results of *ASKDFixed* protocol using typed model option are presented below. As we can see, Cl-AtSe did not find any attacks on any of the security properties of the *ASKDFixed* protocol, which proves that the protocol is safe. The same verification results are obtained by CL-AtSe using untyped model option.

```
SUMMARY      SAFE

DETAILS      BOUNDED_NUMBER_OF_SESSIONS
             TYPED_MODEL
PROTOCOL     /home/span/span/testsuite/results/ASKDFixed.if
```

```
GOAL          As Specified
BACKEND       CL-AtSe
STATISTICS    Analysed   : 24063 states
              Reachable  : 16344 states
              Translation: 0.01 seconds
              Computation: 25.84 seconds
```

5.2   Verification of Complex Transaction Protocols

ChainedTP, presented in Sect. 4.4, is the foundation of *MCCTP* (described in Sect. 4.5). So, to formally verify *MCCTP*, we must formally verify *ChainedTP*. In [7], the correctness of a version of *ChainedTP* was formally demonstrated, in which only the payment gateway was taken into account as entity in making the payments. In this section, we verify *ChainedTP*, which is an extension of the protocol analyzed in [7], taking into consideration, besides the payment gateway, the corresponding banks of the involved entities and their interaction with the payment gateway for performing the payments. In the following, we will detail only the aspects necessary for the formal validation of the *ChainedTP* extension using AVISPA.

We will analyze a *ChainedTP*'s instance with the following participants: the customer C, the broker B_1, the provider P, the payment gateway PG, the customer bank CB, and the broker B_1's bank B_1B. The consideration in *ChainedTP* of the customer bank, respectively, of the broker bank, leads to the addition of two new roles (described below) in the *HLPSL* specification of *ChainedTP*: cbank role corresponding to CB and b1bank role corresponding to B_1B. Also, the essential changes in the behavior of PG are reflected in the transitions of the paygateway role, partially described below.

Figure 5.3 shows the *ChainedTP* execution as a MSC built using the *Protocol Simulation* option from SPAN. The *ChainedTP* execution is a sequence of two subtransactions s_0s_1, where

- s_0 is the subtransaction in which C wants to buy a product from B_1.
- s_1 is the subtransaction in which B_1, to answer C's request, wants to buy the product from P.

The subtransaction s_0 is described by steps 1 and 8–12, while s_1 by steps 2–7. The reception of $PR_{1,2}$ in Step3. from B_1 and sending of $PAR_{1,2}$ to B_1B in Step4. are modeled by the first transition of the paygateway role. PG stores the payment requests he receives in a payment requests list PRList in order to protect against payment requests replay attacks. The reception of $PAR_{1,2}$ in Step4. from PG and sending of $PA_{1,2}$ to PG in Step5. are modeled by the first transition of the b1bank role. The banking system has a payment information list CIList, where both B_1B and CB have access. B_1B checks if B_1 is authorized to use the

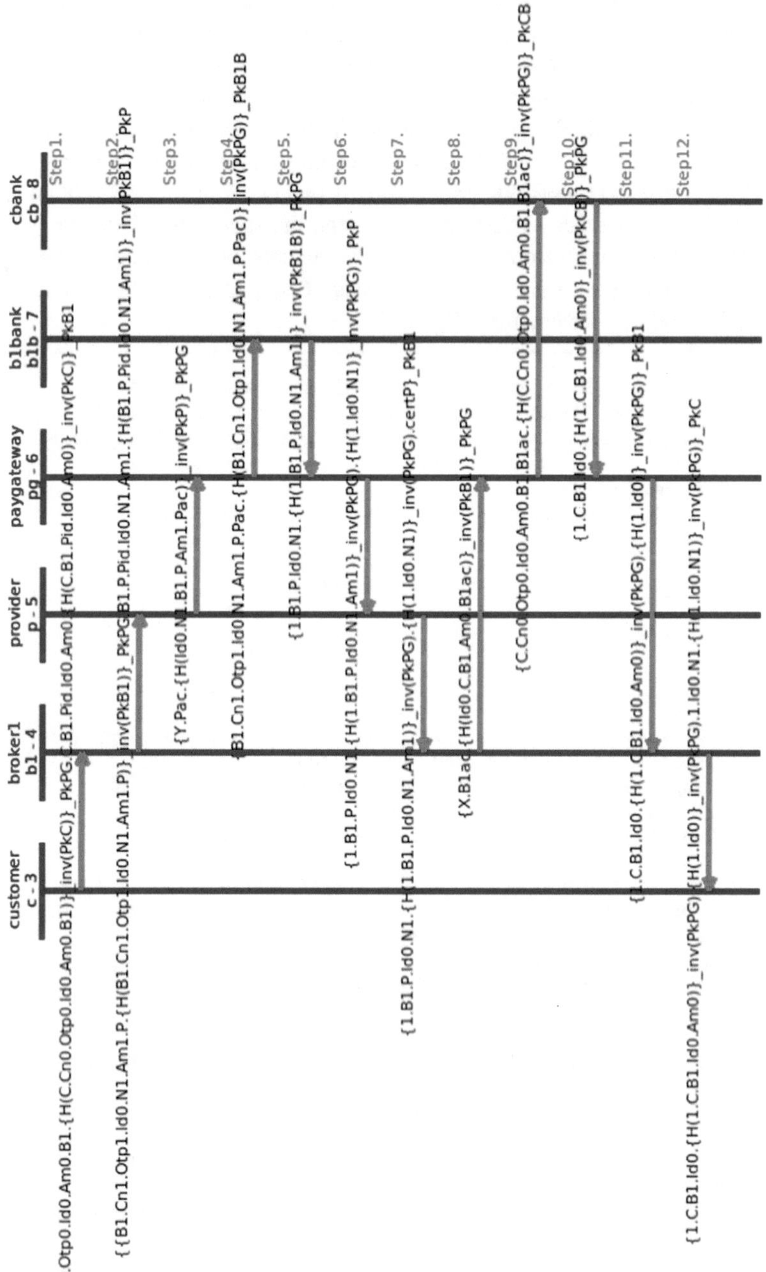

Fig. 5.3 *ChainedTP* simulation in SPAN

card by verifying if CIList contains the payment information B1.Cn1.Otp1 provided by B_1. On successful verification, $B_1 B$ sends a successful $PA_{1,2}$ to PG. A successful or aborted $PA_{i,i+1}/PE_{i,i+1}$ is modeled by the value 1, respectively, 0, in the first component (*Resp*) of $PA_{i,i+1}/PE_{i,i+1}$. The second transition of the paygateway role corresponds to the reception of $PA_{1,2}$ from $B_1 B$ in Step5. and sending of the successful $PE_{1,2}$ to P in Step6. After B_1 receives $PE_{1,2}$ from P in Step7., he continues the subtransaction s_0 by sending $PR_{0,1}$ to PG in Step8. The paygateway role has transitions similar with its first two transitions, to obtain the successful $PA_{0,1}$ from CB in Step10. and to send the successful $PE_{0,1}$ to B_1 in Step11. The first transition from the cbank role models the reception of $PAR_{0,1}$ from PG in Step9. and sending of the successful $PA_{0,1}$ to PG in Step10. In the final step, B_1 sends the successful $PE_{0,1}$ and E_1 to C.

```
role paygateway (C,B1,P,PG: agent, PkC,PkB1,PkP,PkB1B,PkCB,PkPG:
        public_key, PRList: ({agent.text.text.text.text.nat.agent.
        {hash(agent.text.text.text.text.nat.agent)}_inv(public_key)}_
        (public_key).text.{hash(text.text.agent.agent.nat.text)}_
        inv(public_key)) set,
        H: hash_func, Snd,Rcv: channel(dy)) played_by PG def=

local S,Am0,Am1: nat,
      Cn0,Otp0,Cn1,Otp1,Pac,B1ac,Id0,N1,Pid: text

init S := 0

transition

1. S = 0 /\ Rcv({{B1.Cn1'.Otp1'.Id0'.N1'.Am1'.P.{H(B1.Cn1'.Otp1'.Id0'.
   N1'.Am1'.P)}_inv(PkB1)}_PkPG.Pac'.{H(Id0'.N1'.B1.P.Am1'.Pac')}_
   inv(PkP)}_PkPG) /\ not(in({B1.Cn1'.Otp1'.Id0'.N1'.Am1'.P.
   {H(B1.Cn1'.Otp1'.Id0'.N1'.Am1'.P)}_inv(PkB1)}_PkPG.Pac'.
   {H(Id0'.N1'.B1.P.Am1'.Pac')}_inv(PkP), PRList))
   =|>
   S' := 1 /\ PRList' :=cons({B1.Cn1'.Otp1'.Id0'.N1'.Am1'.P.{H(B1.
   Cn1'.Otp1'.Id0'.N1'.Am1'.P)}_inv(PkB1)}_PkPG.Pac'.{H(Id0'.N1'.B1.
   P.Am1'.Pac')}_inv(PkP) , PRList)
   /\ Snd({B1.Cn1'.Otp1'.Id0'.N1'.Am1'.P.Pac'.{H(B1.Cn1'.Otp1'.Id0'.
   N1'.Am1'.P.Pac')}_inv(PkPG)}_PkB1B)
   /\ request(PG,P,pg_p_am1,Am1')

2. S = 1 /\ Rcv({1.B1.P.Id0.N1.{H(1.B1.P.Id0.N1.Am1)}_inv(PkB1B)}_PkPG)
   =|>
   S' :=2 /\ Snd({1.B1.P.Id0.N1.{H(1.B1.P.Id0.N1.Am1)}_inv(PkPG).
   {H(1.Id0.N1)}_inv(PkPG)}_PkP)
   /\ witness(PG,P,p_pg_pe12,1.B1.P.Id0.N1.H(1.B1.P.Id0.N1.Am1).H(1.
   Id0.N1)) /\ witness(PG,B1,b1_pg_pe12,1.B1.P.Id0.N1.H(1.B1.P.Id0.N1.
   Am1).H(1.Id0.N1)) /\ witness(PG,C,c_pg_e1,1.Id0.N1.H(1.Id0.N1))

3. S = 1 /\ Rcv({0.B1.P.Id0.N1.{H(0.B1.P.Id0.N1.Am1)}_inv(PkB1B)}_PkPG)
   =|>
   S' :=3 /\ Snd({0.B1.P.Id0.N1.{H(0.B1.P.Id0.N1.Am1)}_inv(PkPG).{H(0.
   Id0.N1)}_inv(PkPG)}_PkP) /\ witness(PG,P,p_pg_pe12_0,0.B1.P.Id0.N1.
   H(0.B1.P.Id0.N1.Am1).H(0.Id0.N1)) /\ witness(PG,B1,b1_pg_pe12_0,0.
```

```
     B1.P.Id0.N1.H(0.B1.P.Id0.N1.Am1).H(0.Id0.N1))

...
8. S = 10 /\ Rcv({0.C.B1.Id0.{H(0.C.B1.Id0.Am0)}_inv(PkPG).{H(0.Id0)}_
   inv(PkPG).1.B1.P.Id0.N1.{H(1.B1.P.Id0.N1.Am1)}_inv(PkPG).
   {H(1.Id0.N1)}_inv(PkPG)}_PkPG)
   =|>
   S':= 7 /\ Snd({0.C.B1.Id0.{H(0.C.B1.Id0.Am0)}_inv(PkPG).{H(0.Id0)}_
   inv(PkPG).1.B1.P.Id0.N1.{H(1.B1.P.Id0.N1.Am1)}_inv(PkPG).{H(1.Id0.
   N1)}_inv(PkPG)}_PkB1B)

9. S = 7 /\ Rcv({0.B1.P.Id0.N1.{H(0.B1.P.Id0.N1.Am1.1.B1.P.Id0.N1.
   {H(1.B1.P.Id0.N1.Am1)}_inv(PkPG).{H(1.Id0.N1)}_inv(PkPG))}_inv(PkB1B)
   .{H(0.Id0.N1.{H(1.Id0.N1)}_inv(PkPG))}_inv(PkB1B)}_PkPG)
   =|>
   S':= 8 /\ Snd({0.B1.P.Id0.N1.{H(0.B1.P.Id0.N1.Am1.1.B1.P.Id0.N1.
   {H(1.B1.P.Id0.N1.Am1)}_inv(PkPG).{H(1.Id0.N1)}_inv(PkPG))}_inv(PkPG).
   {H(0.Id0.N1.{H(1.Id0.N1)}_inv(PkPG))}_inv(PkPG)}_PkB1)
   /\ Snd({0.B1.P.Id0.N1.{H(0.B1.P.Id0.N1.Am1.1.B1.P.Id0.N1.
   {H(1.B1.P.Id0.N1.Am1)}_inv(PkPG).{H(1.Id0.N1)}_inv(PkPG))}_inv(PkPG).
   {H(0.Id0.N1.{H(1.Id0.N1)}_inv(PkPG))}_inv(PkPG)}_PkP)
   /\ witness(PG,P,p_pg_ape12,0.B1.P.Id0.N1.H(0.B1.P.Id0.N1.Am1.1.B1.P.
     Id0.N1.H(1.B1.P.Id0.N1.Am1).H(1.Id0.N1)).H(0.Id0.N1.H(1.Id0.N1)))
   /\ witness(PG,B1,b1_pg_ape12,0.B1.P.Id0.N1.H(0.B1.P.Id0.N1.Am1.1.B1.
     P.Id0.N1.H(1.B1.P.Id0.N1.Am1).H(1.Id0.N1)).H(0.Id0.N1.H(1.Id0.N1)))

...
end role

role b1bank (B1,P,PG,B1B: agent, PkPG,PkB1B: public_key,
       CIList: (agent.text.text) set, H: hash_func,
       Snd, Rcv: channel(dy)) played_by B1B def=

local S,Am0,Am1: nat,
      C: agent,
      Cn1,Otp1,Pac,Id0,N1: text

init S := 0

transition

1. S = 0 /\ Rcv({B1.Cn1'.Otp1'.Id0'.N1'.Am1'.P.Pac'.{H(B1.Cn1'.Otp1'.
   Id0'.N1'.Am1'.P.Pac')}_inv(PkPG)}_PkB1B)
   /\ in(B1.Cn1'.Otp1' , CIList)
   =|>
   S' := 1
   /\ Snd({1.B1.P.Id0'.N1'.{H(1.B1.P.Id0'.N1'.Am1')}_inv(PkB1B)}_PkPG)
   /\ request(B1B,B1,b1b_b1_pi1,B1.Cn1'.Otp1'.Id0'.N1'.Am1'.P)

2. S = 0 /\ Rcv({B1.Cn1'.Otp1'.Id0'.N1'.Am1'.P.Pac'.{H(B1.Cn1'.Otp1'.
   Id0'.N1'.Am1'.P.Pac')}_inv(PkPG)}_PkB1B)
   /\ not(in(B1.Cn1'.Otp1' , CIList))
   =|>
   S' := 2
   /\ Snd({0.B1.P.Id0'.N1'.{H(0.B1.P.Id0'.N1'.Am1')}_inv(PkB1B)}_PkPG)

3. S = 1 /\ Rcv({0.C'.B1.Id0.{H(0.C'.B1.Id0.Am0')}_inv(PkPG).
```

```
          {H(0.Id0)}_inv(PkPG).1.B1.P.Id0.N1.{H(1.B1.P.Id0.N1.Am1)}_inv(PkPG)
          .{H(1.Id0.N1)}_inv(PkPG)}_PkB1B)
          =|>
          S' := 3
          /\ Snd({0.B1.P.Id0.N1.{H(0.B1.P.Id0.N1.Am1.1.B1.P.Id0.N1.{H(1.B1.P.
          Id0.N1.Am1)}_inv(PkPG).{H(1.Id0.N1)}_inv(PkPG))}_inv(PkB1B).
          {H(0.Id0.N1.{H(1.Id0.N1)}_inv(PkPG))}_inv(PkB1B)}_PkPG)

  end role

  role cbank (C,B1,PG,CB: agent, PkPG,PkCB: public_key,
          CIList: (agent.text.text) set, H: hash_func,
          Snd, Rcv: channel(dy)) played_by CB def=

  local S,Am0: nat,
          Cn0,Otp0,B1ac,Id0: text

  init S := 0

  transition

  1. S = 0 /\ Rcv({C.Cn0'.Otp0'.Id0'.Am0'.B1.B1ac'.{H(C.Cn0'.Otp0'.Id0'.
          Am0'.B1.B1ac')}_inv(PkPG)}_PkCB)
          /\ in(C.Cn0'.Otp0' , CIList)
          =|>
          S' := 1
          /\ Snd({1.C.B1.Id0'.{H(1.C.B1.Id0'.Am0')}_inv(PkCB)}_PkPG)
          /\ request(CB,C,cb_c_pi0,C.Cn0'.Otp0'.Id0'.Am0'.B1)

  2. S = 0 /\ Rcv({C.Cn0'.Otp0'.Id0'.Am0'.B1.B1ac'.{H(C.Cn0'.Otp0'.Id0'.
          Am0'.B1.B1ac')}_inv(PkPG)}_PkCB)
          /\ not(in(C.Cn0'.Otp0' , CIList))
          =|>
          S' := 2
          /\ Snd({0.C.B1.Id0'.{H(0.C.B1.Id0'.Am0')}_inv(PkCB)}_PkPG)

    end role
```

MSC from Fig. 5.3 shows the *ChainedTP* execution for the scenario in which both subtransactions s_0 and s_1 are successful. Next, we will discuss how some interesting scenarios of *ChainedTP* are modeled, in which the abortion of one of the subtransactions leads to the abortion of the entire chained transaction, preserving fairness.

The *Protocol Simulation* option can be also used to obtain MSC from Fig. 5.4 describing the behavior of *ChainedTP* in a scenario in which *Resolution 1* sub-protocol is applied. As we can see, the subtransaction s_1 is successful, so Steps1–9. from Fig. 5.4 are the same with Steps1–9. from Fig. 5.3. The reception of $PAR_{0,1}$ in Step9. and sending of an aborted $PA_{0,1}$ in Step10. are modeled by the second transition of the cbank role. In this case, we consider a scenario in which the payment information C.Cn0.Otp0 provided by C is not valid, because it is not found by CB in CIList. Thus, the verification of C's authentication fails, and CB sends an aborted $PA_{0,1}$ to PG. When B_1 receives the aborted $PE_{0,1}$

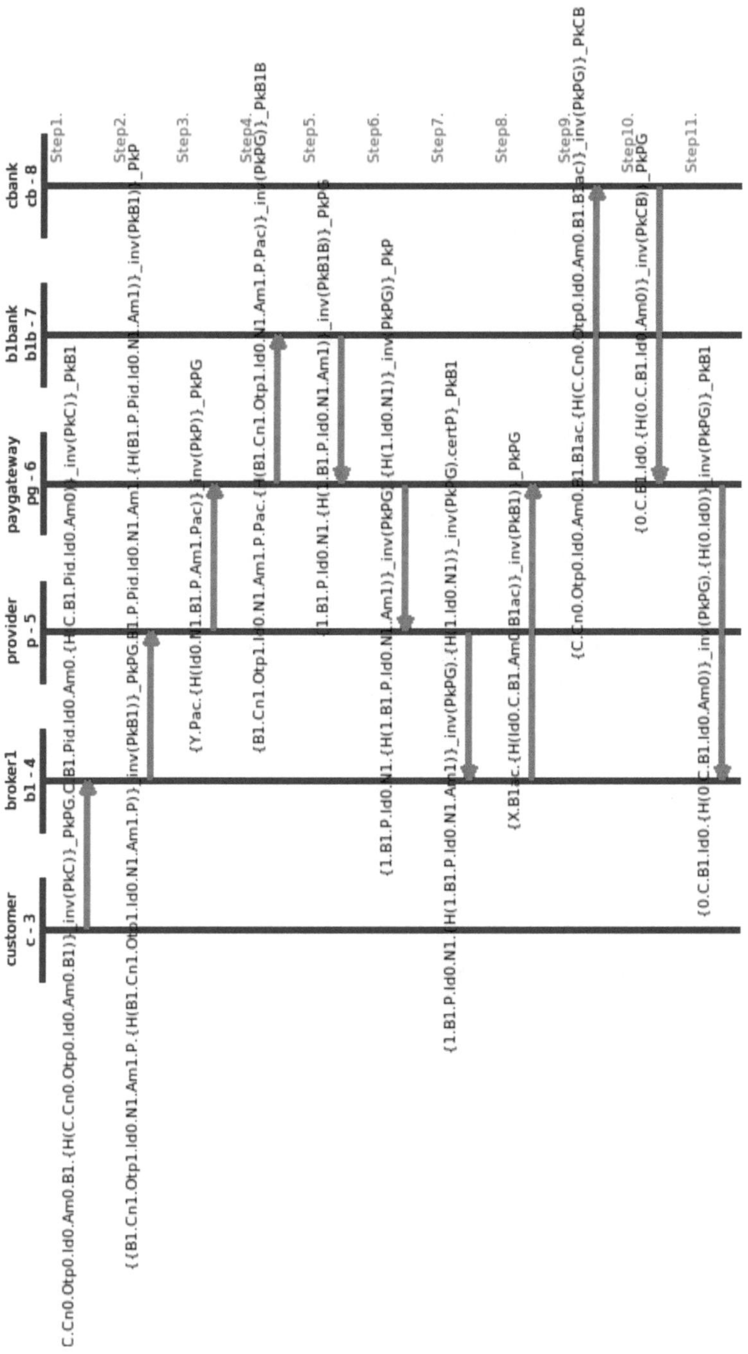

Fig. 5.4 *Resolution 1 sub-protocol using Protocol Simulation in SPAN*

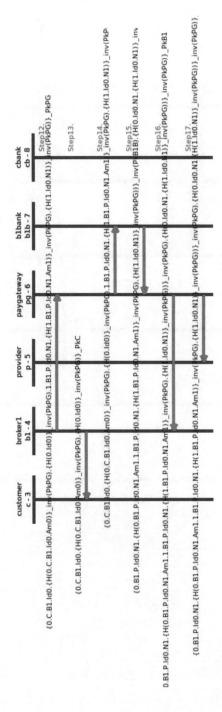

Fig. 5.4 (continued)

(Step11.), he initiates the *Resolution 1* sub-protocol (Step12.). Transition 8 from the paygateway role models the reception from B_1 of aborted $PE_{0,1}$ and successful $PE_{1,2}$ in Step12. and sends them to B_1B for $PE_{1,2}$ abortion in Step14. In transition 3 from b1bank role, B_1B generates $AAPE_{1,2}$ to abort $PE_{1,2}$ and sends it to PG in Step15. Transition 9 from the paygateway role corresponds to the reception of $AAPE_{1,2}$ from B_1B and sending of $APE_{1,2}$ to B_1 and P in Steps16. and 17.

An interesting scenario, in which *Resolution 2* sub-protocol is applied, is described by MSC from Fig. 5.5 obtained using *Intruder Simulation* option. In Steps2–7., B_1 and P obtain the successful $PE_{1,2}$ corresponding to the success of the subtransaction s_1. After B_1 receives the aborted $PE_{0,1}$ corresponding to s_0 (Step11.), he sends it to C. However, this transmission cannot reach the intended destination C because the intruder blocks it (Step12.). In this case, C waits until the timeout expires, and then he initiates *Resolution 2* sub-protocol in Step14. PG responds to C with the aborted $PE_{0,1}$ (Step15.), and *ChainedTP* continues with *Resolution 1* sub-protocol initiated by B_1 to abort the subtransaction s_1.

Typically, a `session` role defines a *ChainedTP*'s session by parallel composition of `customer`, `broker1`, `provider`, `paygateway`, `b1bank`, and `cbank` roles. We verify a protocol scenario similar to the one analyzed in [7], defined by parallel composition of four *ChainedTP*'s sessions: a session played by honest agents and three sessions in which the intruder plays the `customer`, `broker1`, and `provider` role, respectively.

In Table 5.2, we present the security goals of *ChainedTP* modeled in *HLPSL*. The first column in Table 5.2 describes the security property we want to verify, and the second column shows how the corresponding security property is specified in *HLPSL*. Each strong authentication property requires two corresponding goal facts `witness` and `request` that uses the protocol identifier specified by `authentication` on keyword. For example, the specification of the strong authentication of B_1 to B_1B on PI_1 requires the goal fact `witness(B1,B1B,b1b_b1_pi1,B1.Cn1.Otp1.Id0'.N1'.Am1.P)` in the first transition of the `broker1` role and a corresponding goal fact `request(B1B,B1,b1b_b1_pi1,B1.Cn1'.Otp1'.Id0'.N1'.Am1'.P)` in the first transition of the `b1bank` role. To specify the strong authentication of PG on different payment evidences, we will use different protocol identifiers, depending on the transitions in which these are performed. For example, the identifier `b1_pg_pe12` / `b1_pg_pe12_0` / `b1_pg_ape12` is used to specify the strong authentication of PG to B_1 on successful/aborted/aborted after successful $PE_{1,2}$.

Strong fairness, non-repudiation, and integrity are specified by strong authentication goals. Thus, strong fairness is modeled by the strong authentication of PG on the subtransaction's payment evidences. Non-repudiation regarding some entity is obtained by the strong authentication of that entity on relevant information. Integrity of PI_i and $PE_{i,i+1}$ is guaranteed by the strong authentication of B_i on PI_i and the strong authentication of PG on $PE_{i,i+1}$, respectively.

The verification results of *ChainedTP* using typed model option are presented below. As we can see, Cl-AtSe did not find any attacks on any of the security

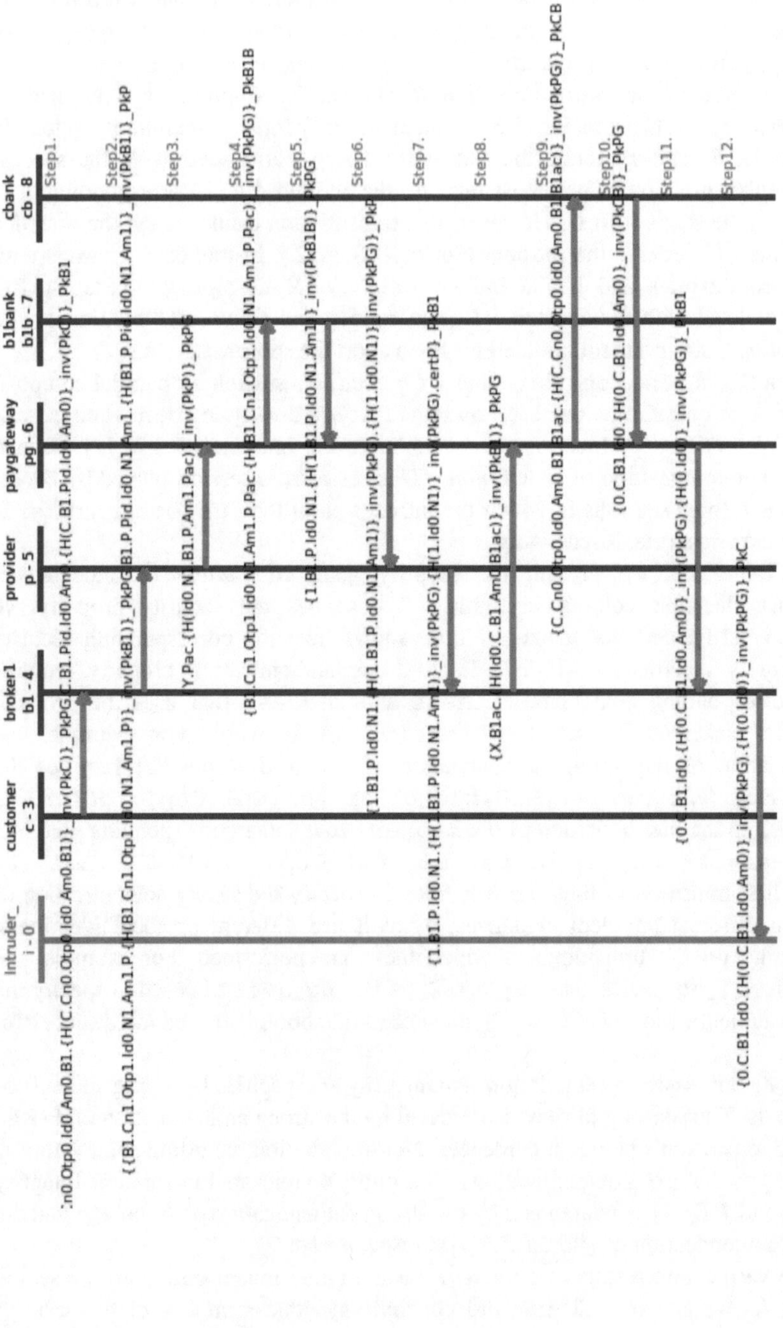

Fig. 5.5 *Resolution 2 sub-protocol using Intruder Simulation* in SPAN

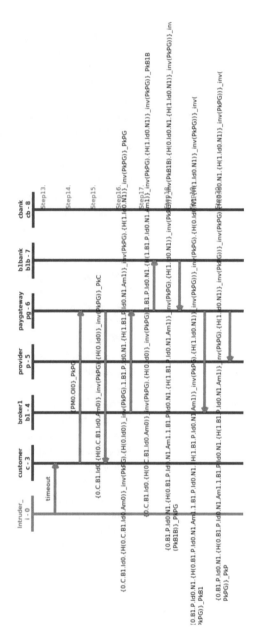

Fig. 5.5 (continued)

Table 5.2 Security goals in *ChainedTP*

Property	Specification
Confidentiality of Cn_0	`secret(Cn0,scn,{C,PG,CB})`
Confidentiality of Cn_1	`secret(Cn1,scn1,{B1,PG,B1B})`
Strong mutual authentication between C and B_1 on OI_0	`authentication_on b1_c_oi0,` `c_b1_oi0`
Strong mutual authentication between B_1 and P on OI_1	`authentication_on p_b1_oi1` `authentication_on b1_p_oi1`
Strong authentication of B_1 to B_1B on PI_1	`authentication_on b1b_b1_pi1`
Strong authentication of C to CB on PI_0	`authentication_on cb_c_pi0`
Strong authentication of P to PG on Am_1	`authentication_on pg_p_am1`
Strong authentication of B_1 to PG on Am_0	`authentication_on pg_b1_am0`
Strong authentication of PG to P on $PE_{1,2}$	`authentication_on p_pg_pe12,` `p_pg_pe12_0, p_pg_ape12`
Strong authentication of PG to B_1 on $PE_{1,2}$ and $PE_{0,1}$	`authentication_on b1_pg_pe12,` `b1_pg_pe12_0, b1_pg_ape12,` `b1_pg_pe01, b1_pg_pe01_0`
Strong authentication of PG to C on $PE_{0,1}$ and E_1	`authentication_on c_pg_pe01,` `c_pg_pe01_0, c_pg_e1`
Strong fairness	Strong authentication of: PG to P on $PE_{1,2}$, PG to B_1 on $PE_{1,2}$ and $PE_{0,1}$, PG to C on $PE_{0,1}$ and E_1, and $PE_{1,2}$, $PE_{0,1}$ have the same response
Non-repudiation regarding C	Strong authentication of C to CB on PI_0
Non-repudiation regarding B_1 in s_1	Strong authentication of B_1 to B_1B on PI_1
Non-repudiation regarding B_1 in s_0	Strong authentication of B_1 to PG on Am_0
Non-repudiation regarding P	Strong authentication of P to PG on Am_1
Integrity of PI_0	Strong authentication of C to CB on PI_0
Integrity of PI_1	Strong authentication of B_1 to B_1B on PI_1
Integrity of $PE_{1,2}$	Strong authentication of: PG to P on $PE_{1,2}$ PG to B_1 on $PE_{1,2}$
Integrity of $PE_{0,1}$	Strong authentication of: PG to B_1 on $PE_{0,1}$ PG to C on $PE_{0,1}$

properties of the *ChainedTP* from Table 5.2, which proves that the protocol is safe. The high number of analyzed states highlights the complexity of *ChainedTP*.

```
SUMMARY      SAFE

DETAILS      BOUNDED_NUMBER_OF_SESSIONS
             TYPED_MODEL
PROTOCOL     /home/span/span/testsuite/results/ChainedTP.if
GOAL         As Specified
BACKEND      CL-AtSe
STATISTICS   Analysed    : 1067697601 states
             Reachable   : 69155703 states
             Translation: 1.46 seconds
             Computation: 21247.94 seconds
```

References

1. Armando, A., et al.: The AVISPA tool for the automated validation of internet security protocols and applications. In: Etessami, K., Rajamani, S.K. (eds.) Computer Aided Verification. CAV 2005. Lecture Notes in Computer Science, vol. 3576. Springer, Berlin, Heidelberg (2005). https://doi.org/10.1007/11513988_27
2. Armando, A., Compagna, L.: SATMC: A SAT-based model checker for security protocols. In: Alferes, J.J., Leite, J. (eds.) Logics in Artificial Intelligence. JELIA 2004. Lecture Notes in Computer Science, vol. 3229. Springer, Berlin, Heidelberg (2004). https://doi.org/10.1007/978-3-540-30227-8_68
3. AVISPA Team: AVISPA v1.1 User Manual. Version: 1.1 (2006). SPAN + AVISPA Distribution. http://people.irisa.fr/Thomas.Genet/span/. Cited June 25, 2022
4. AVISPA Team: HLPSL Tutorial: A Beginner's Guide to Modelling and Analysing Internet Security Protocols. Version: 1.1 (2006). SPAN + AVISPA Distribution. http://people.irisa.fr/Thomas.Genet/span/. Cited June 25, 2022
5. Basin, D., Modersheim, S., Vigano, L.: OFMC: a symbolic model-checker for security protocols. Int. J. Inform. Secur. **4**, 181–208 (2005). https://doi.org/10.1007/s10207-004-0055-7
6. Bella, G.: Formal Correctness of Security Protocols. Springer, Berlin (2007)
7. Bîrjoveanu, C.V., Bîrjoveanu, M.: Chained transaction protocol automated verification using Cl-AtSe. In: Obaidat, M.S., Ben-Othman, J. (eds.) E-Business and Telecommunications. ICETE 2020. Communications in Computer and Information Science, vol. 1484. Springer, Cham (2021). https://doi.org/10.1007/978-3-030-90428-9_9
8. Blanchet, B.: An efficient cryptographic protocol verifier based on prolog rules. In: 14th IEEE Computer Security Foundations Workshop, pp. 82–96 (2001). https://doi.org/10.1109/CSFW.2001.930138
9. Boichut, Y., Héam, P.-C., Kouchnarenko, O.: Automatic Verification of Security Protocols Using Approximations. Research Report RR-5727, INRIA (2005)
10. Chevalier, Y., Compagna, L., Cuellar, J., Hankes Drielsma, P., Mantovani, J., Mödersheim, S., Vigneron, L.: A high level protocol specification language for industrial security-sensitive protocols. In: Workshop on Specification and Automated Processing of Security Requirements, Austrian Computer Society, pp. 193–205 (2004)

11. Clifford Neuman, B., Ts'o, T.: Kerberos: an authentication service for computer networks. IEEE Commun. **32**(9), 33–38 (1994)
12. Cremers, C.J.F.: The Scyther tool: verification, falsification, and analysis of security protocols. In: Gupta, A., Malik, S. (eds.) Computer Aided Verification. CAV 2008. Lecture Notes in Computer Science, vol. 5123. Springer, Berlin, Heidelberg (2008). https://doi.org/10.1007/ 978-3-540-70545-1_38
13. Cremers, C., Mauw, S.: Operational Semantics and Verification of Security Protocols. Information Security and Cryptography Series. Springer, Berlin (2012)
14. Dolev, D., Yao, A.: On the Security of Public-Key Protocols. IEEE Trans. Inform. Theory **2**(29), 198–208 (1983). https://doi.org/10.1109/TIT.1983.1056650
15. Glouche, Y., Genet, T., Houssay, E.: SPAN: A Security Protocol ANimator for AVISPA. User Manual. IRISA/Université de Rennes 1 (2008)
16. Heen, O., Genet, T., Geller, S., Prigent, N.: An industrial and academic joint experiment on automated verification of a security protocol. In: Proceedings of the IFIP Networking Workshop on Mobile and Networks Security, pp. 39–53 (2008)
17. Lamport, L.: The temporal logic of actions. ACM Trans. Program. Lang. Syst. **16**(3), 872–923 (1994)
18. Lowe, G.: A hierarchy of authentication specifications. In: Proceedings 10th Computer Security Foundations Workshop, pp. 31–43 (1997). https://doi.org/10.1109/CSFW.1997.596782
19. Lowe, G.: Casper: a compiler for the analysis of security protocols. J. Comput. Secur. **6**(1–2), 53–84 (1998)
20. Meier, S., Schmidt, B., Cremers, C., Basin, D.: The TAMARIN prover for the symbolic analysis of security protocols. In: Sharygina, N., Veith, H. (eds.) Computer Aided Verification. CAV 2013. Lecture Notes in Computer Science, vol. 8044. Springer, Berlin, Heidelberg (2013). https://doi.org/10.1007/978-3-642-39799-8_48
21. Paulson, L.C.: The inductive approach to verifying cryptographic protocols. J. Comput. Secur. **6**(1–2), 85–128 (1998)
22. Ryan, P., Schneider, S., Goldsmith, M., Lowe, G., Roscoe, A.: Modelling and Analysis of Security Protocols. Addison-Wesley, Reading (2000)
23. SPAN, a Security Protocol ANimator for AVISPA. http://people.irisa.fr/Thomas.Genet/span/ Cited June 25, 2022
24. Turuani, M.: The CL-Atse protocol analyser. In: 17th International Conference on Rewriting Techniques and Applications, LNCS, vol. 4098, pp. 277–286. Springer, Berlin (2006). https:// doi.org/10.1007/11805618_21
25. Vigano, L.: Automated security protocol analysis with the AVISPA tool. Electronic Notes in Theoretical Computer Science, vol. 155, pp. 61–86 (2006). https://doi.org/10.1016/j.entcs. 2005.11.052

Chapter 6
Conclusions

This book presents the state of the art for two-party and for multi-party fair exchange protocols and provides insight details regarding multi-party fair exchange e-commerce protocols for buying physical products in scenarios involving complex, chained transactions and their combination.

As we can see in Sect. 2.1, much attention was given to two-party e-commerce protocols. Although there are solutions for multi-party scenarios with applications in contract signing, non-repudiation, and certified email, the solutions developed for multi-party e-commerce scenarios are only few and appeared much later. One of the main challenges in designing secure multi-party e-commerce protocols is that the protocols that consider only one customer and one merchant are not appropriate and cannot be easily extended to multi-party scenarios. To capture as accurately as possible the online shopping needs of the customer, we introduce in this book complex e-commerce transactions as a combination in any form of aggregate, optional, and partial transactions. Also, we tackle the cases in which, in a chain transaction, the customer shops online for a physical product from a provider through many intermediaries. Furthermore, we provide a multi-party e-commerce protocol for mixing complex and chained transactions.

The difficulty of designing secure multi-party e-commerce protocols resides in multiple participants (customer, merchants, intermediaries, providers), the bundle nature of the goods purchased by the customer, and in the fact that some essential security requirements from two-party e-commerce scenarios are not preserved in multi-party e-commerce scenarios. Thus, we readjust strong fairness, effectiveness, and timeliness for multi-party scenarios for complex, chained transactions and their combination in Sects. 3.3 and 4.3.

To have a starting point and an overview regarding the current solutions developed for e-commerce, we provided the state of the art regarding two-party and multi-party e-commerce protocols. We presented in detail multi-party solutions ensuring strong fairness for e-commerce complex transactions (*CTP* in Chap. 3), chained transactions (*ChainedTP* in Chap. 4), and their combination (*MCCTP*

© The Author(s), under exclusive license to Springer Nature Switzerland AG 2022
C. V. Bîrjoveanu, M. Bîrjoveanu, *Secure Multi-Party E-Commerce Protocols*,
SpringerBriefs in Computer Science, https://doi.org/10.1007/978-3-030-99351-1_6

in Chap. 4). A multi-party e-commerce solution (*CTPCP*) providing customer's privacy in transactions including physical products delivery is detailed in Chap. 3.

One of the goals of the book is to design efficient multi-party e-commerce protocols. Thus, in all the multi-party e-commerce protocols presented in detail in this book (*CTP*, *CTPCP*, *ChainedTP*, and *MCCTP*), the involvement of *TTP* is minimal. In *CTP*, *ChainedTP*, and *MCCTP*, we considered that the payment gateway *PG* is *TTP*. If in these protocols the participants behave honestly, then *PG* does not act as *TTP*, but only as an interface between merchant/broker/provider and the customer's bank/broker's bank. Considering *PG* as offline *TTP* brings more benefits. Firstly, *PG* is a component of the banking system that has a high level of trust, so implementing a multi-party protocol in which *PG* is an offline *TTP* has low costs. Secondly, if disputes arise, strong fairness is obtained with reduced effort because *PG* has the payment evidences needed to solve the disputes. Thirdly, the load on the customer is reduced given the fact that the customer downloads the payment Web segment digitally signed by *PG*, so any action is realized by payment Web segment in the name of the customer. Thus, the customer only needs the digital certificate of *PG*'s public key to validate the payment Web segment. In the multi-party e-commerce protocols for complex transactions, the payment Web segment builds a transaction tree associated with the complex transaction. We choose for the transaction tree a structure suitable both for representing a complex transaction (different transaction types—optional, aggregate, and partial; variable number of products in any type of transaction) and for the efficient access to its different components.

Next, we will measure the overhead regarding the number of messages from *CTP*, *ChainedTP*, and *MCCTP* when the participants behave honestly. The maximum number of messages in *CTP* is $6n$, where n is the number of products in the complex transaction; in *ChainedTP*, it is $6m$, where $m-1$ is the number of brokers in the chained transaction; and in *MCCTP*, it is $6nm$. As we can see, the number of messages is proportional with the complexity introduced by the transaction type. We remark that the overload introduced by *ChainedTP/MCCTP* compared to *CTP* regarding the size of messages is given only by E_i component from each payment evidence $PE_{i,i+1}$ corresponding to each subtransaction s_i from the chain. In Table 6.1, we analyze the number of cryptographic operations (signature, verification of signature, hybrid encryption, and decryption) performed by each kind of participant in multi-party e-commerce protocols, when he behaves honestly. We observe that in *MCCTP*, the number of cryptographic operations needed depends on the ones from *CTP* and *ChainedTP*, being determined by multiplication between the number of products from the complex transaction and the maximum numbers of operations from all instances of *ChainedTP* executed in *MCCTP*. We consider that in these protocols, the number of messages and their size, the number of cryptographic operations is the minimum needed to achieve authentication/authorization, strong fairness, effectiveness, non-repudiation, confidentiality, and integrity.

CTP, *ChainedTP* and *MCCTP* are formally verified using AVISPA. Chapter 5 describes AVISPA tool and presents the formal verification of *ChainedTP*. As

Table 6.1 Comparison of the number of cryptographic operations for each kind of participant in multi-party e-commerce protocols

Operation	Signature			Verification			Encryption			Decryption		
Protocols	*P1*	*P2*	*P3*	*P1*	*P2*	*P3*	*P1*	*P2*	*P3*	*P1*	*P2*	*P3*
Customer	2n	2	2n	n	3	3n	2n	2	2n	n	1	n
Merchant	r	-	-	2r	-	-	2r	-	-	2r	-	-
Broker	-	3	3b	-	5	5b	-	4	4b	-	3	3b
Provider	-	1	p	-	2	2p	-	2	2p	-	2	2p
Payment Gateway	2n	3m	3mn	3n	3m	3mn	2n	2m	2mn	3n	3m	3mn
Customer Bank	n	1	n	n	1	n	n	1	n	n	1	n
Broker Bank	b	1	b	b	1	b	b	1	b	b	1	b

P1 = CTP
P2 = ChainedTP
P3 = MCCTP
n = the number of products in the complex transaction
r = the number of subtransactions (exchanges) in which the merchant is involved in *CTP*
b = the number of subtransactions in which the broker is involved in all chained transactions in *MCCTP*
p = the number of subtransactions in which the provider is involved in *MCCTP*
m-1 = the number of brokers in *ChainedTP* = the maximum number of brokers involved in any chained transaction from *MCCTP*
- = N.A.

a result of this verification, *MCCTP* is also validated because it is based on *ChainedTP*.

The multi-party e-commerce protocol *CTPCP* presented in Chap. 3 for physical products delivery is the first protocol that ensures customer's privacy using an offline *TTP*. The main goal of *CTPCP* is to guarantee the privacy of the customer considering the physical products delivery, so the infrastructure required by it is more complex and different compared to the one needed for *CTP*, *ChainedTP*, and *MCCTP*. *TTP* in *CTPCP* can be a component of the banking system agreed by all banks in the similar manner as *PG* in the other protocols (*CTP*, *ChainedTP*, and *MCCTP*).

The multi-party e-commerce protocols detailed in this book are distinguished by the following:

- Are based on existing architectures which uses the payment gateway (*CTP ChainedTP*, *MCCTP*) or on existing architectures in which the physical delivery of products uses password lockers (*CTPCP*)
- Payment gateway is used as offline *TTP*
- Applicability in various e-business models
- Formally validated

Therefore, we believe that these protocols are suitable to be adopted in practice.

Printed in the United States
by Baker & Taylor Publisher Services